HOW TO RESTORE
Paintwork

OSPREY
RESTORATION
GUIDE 4

HOW TO RESTORE
Paintwork

Miles Wilkins

Published in 1984 by Osprey Publishing Limited
12–14 Long Acre, London WC2E 9LP
Member company of the George Philip Group
First reprint autumn 1984
Second reprint spring 1985

Sole distributors for the USA

Osceola, Wisconsin 54020, USA

British Library Cataloguing in Publication Data

Wilkins, Miles
    How to restore car paintwork.—(Restoration
    series)
    1. Automobiles—Painting
    I. Title   II. Series
    629.2′6′0288   TL154
ISBN 0-85045-557-X

Editor Tim Parker
Associate Graham Robson
Design Gwyn Lewis

Filmset and printed by
BAS Printers Limited, Over Wallop, Stockbridge, Hampshire

CONTENTS

Introduction

In the writing of this book I hope I have succeeded in giving an insight into the complexities of painting and spraying. As with all skills, spraying perhaps takes the longest to acquire and learn and to understand all the faults that can and do arise. If you are undertaking spraying for the first time, please realise that the finish cannot hope to be as good as the professional can make it, but by reading this book I hope you may be able to be proud of your result. With any painting, treat it as the 'icing on the cake'; do make sure the repairs are carried out correctly, especially on GRP bodies, otherwise it doesn't matter how good the final coats are, for all the blemishes underneath will show through. There is no doubt that a first class spray makes the car stand out and my only regret in this book is that I am limited to black and white photography, which cannot of course show the differences in various painting stages, and some of the wonderful paintwork finishes achieved.

I am indebted to my wife for taking all the photographs, to Ian Symms of Fibreglass Services and to Philip Peet and David Lander of Autobodies, Tangmere, Chichester, without whom the completion of this book would not have been possible.

My thanks go also to Derek Hammond of Chandler and Hammond, Chichester; Keith Shelfer; ICI; International; and to Dilys Simmons for typing the manuscript.

Miles Wilkins
May 1984

Chapter 1 | Paint systems and associated products

The prime function of paint is to protect, and whilst doing so it may as well be colourful. If this did not apply, all vehicles could be sprayed with underseal to achieve the same degree of protection. However, with all the brainwashing about car paint treatments, why do they still rust? At present there are no sensible alternatives to painting, although the increased use of plastics could make this a possibility in the future, but then fashion would dictate that these be colour coded to match the rest of the cosmetic treatment. Citroën, with their BX model, have used plastics extensively for body panels, Saab and Volvo use galvanised metal shields on the underside of their wheelarches and the much-publicised Delorean did away with paint by using stainless steel body panels. Even Pressed Steel introduced their Zincote body that would never rust in the late 1950s, but this never came to fruition.

Colours, too, have changed. Gone are the days when black seemed to be the only 'colour'—not strictly true, because since the advent of the motor car there have always been the 'natural' colours of red, blue, yellow and white. It was Henry Ford who decided black was *de rigeur* because it was far easier and cheaper to paint a whole assembly line of cars one colour, rather than to employ several different paint colours. Colours match the mood of society too. After the First World War and the Depression the mood was dark, and car colours reflected this—black, dark greys, blues and maroons were normal. Britain's own racing colour was British racing green, hardly the gaudiness of Italian red, Belgian yellow and German white (later silver) or French light blue.

After the Second World War new cars (except in the

USA) were scarce and colours were still fairly sombre, but with the prospect of easier times ahead, coupled with great advances in synthetic dyes (i.e. pigments) new bright colours appeared on cars. Metallics were offered in the fifties, Aston Martin being one of the first users. The trend has continued up to the present day, for there are literally hundreds of different colours to choose from, metallics or solid colour, and ironically if black is now what you want, you may even have to pay extra for it!

What is paint? As used in the motor industry, it is a liquid that dries in a coloured or clear film (lacquer) on a surface. All paints contain pigments—the particles that give the colour—and these can be natural or man-made. For metallics aluminium particles (fleck) are added in varying grades to determine the coarseness of the overall effect.

Binders are agents which hold the pigment particles together and allow the paint layer to form an even film. They also provide the adhesion to the preceding layer. Finally there is the solvent which is the paint/binder carrier.

The pigments are suspended in the solvent (thinners) when applied, the solvent evaporates leaving the hardened pigment/binder film on the surface. Solvents are varied and range from water (household emulsion) to alcohols, and petroleum distillates. Paint solvents are usually highly volatile.

Paint systems are extremely difficult to understand— more often than not, one scheme can go under three different names—although I will outline all the systems and names, I will start by simplifying the main paint systems that can be used by anybody.

1   Cellulose—most people know this type. The full title is Nitro cellulose lacquers. Paint is thinned down with the solvent, mixed 50–50, then sprayed, and polished to a high degree of gloss. Easy for spot repairs, blow-ins and ideal for the first time sprayer, for any mistake can easily be rectified. As a high content of solvent is used, the covering power is not ideal and so a high usage of paint is required. Cellulose is not as flexible as the later 'plastic' paints, and will dull with age if not kept polished.

2   Synthetic Enamel. This is an air-drying enamel based on man-made resins, with drying oils added. Minimal solvent is

required, and the paint covers with one or two coats to give a plastic film on the surface. Drying time takes up to 16–20 hours at 20 degrees C (68 degrees F), but is touch dry in up to four hours. Not really recommended for the beginner. If a mistake occurs, the whole panel has to be re-done. One cannot 'spot repair' because the second application will just sit on the first, and being a plastic film it will not blend in as cellulose does. Tough and durable, flexible in service, you get good gloss straight from the spray gun. More economical than cellulose, as less is used. Although polishing can be done it is not recommended until the surface is at least a few months old.

3   Two-pack acrylic enamels contain acrylic and melamine resins (man made) and when mixed with a hardener (hence 'two pack') will give all the attributes of an air drying enamel, but will harden off much quicker at any given temperature. The hardener contains isocyanate and when sprayed the vapour is lethal, so external breathing apparatus must be used, with a different, clean air supply, and for this reason alone the novice should not use this system.

The major car manufacturers now use acrylic enamels that harden under a high temperature bake. The resins in them reform and flow uniformly, or reset to give the tough high gloss finish.

One system is TSA—thermosetting acrylic—which is used for solid colour and metallics. Here resins set together at 130 degrees C. At this temperature high bake time is 30 minutes.

Another system is TPA—thermoplastic acrylic—whereby the resins re-flow at 160 degrees C, and is used for solid colour and metallics.

Finally a third system, used for solid colour only, is a high bake synthetic enamel. It requires 30 minutes at 130 degrees C to harden off fully.

Other paint finishes available, apart from the three mentioned, are:

1   Acrylic lacquers, based on acrylic resins and plasticising agents. This requires no hardener and dries by solvent evaporation. Used in solid and metallic colours.

Base coat and clear systems are acrylic lacquer paints. Can be polished to a high degree of gloss. Cellulose and acrylic paints are very similar in application, with acrylic systems having a harder and more durable finish than cellulose. Lotus Cars use

Above and opposite **A self-contained spray-bake oven, used for all low-bake applications. The temperature reaches up to 80 degrees C (175 degrees F). Note the air filtration/heat unit above the car, and the arrangement of lighting, which gives shadow-free illumination. The operator of this oven turns round six vehicles every day**

this system for their current (1984) metallic finishes.

2   Low bake enamels. These come to full hardness in an oven at lower temperatures than the high bake systems (TSA and TPA). Temperature used is around 80 degrees C (175 degrees F). The end result is a very high gloss, extremely tough and durable in service. The finish requires no polishing. It must **not** be used on GRP bodies as the temperatures involved are too high and resin deformation will result.

3   Air-dry synthetic enamels and hardener. This is a standard air-dry finish that can be brought up to a 'two-pack' specification. Shortens drying time, and these finishes can be low-baked as well. Finish will not be as hard as a true low-bake enamel.

4   Brushing cellulose. This has almost died out now, but was the mainstay of the prewar paint industry. Brushing cellulose is a brush-applied nitrocellulose lacquer, which dries over a period of time by solvent evaporation. Preparation has to be

meticulous and each coat has to be flatted down prior to the next application. After the final coats, the finish is burnished to a high degree of gloss. If properly applied, the result is indistinguishable from a spray gun and the depth of shine is far greater.

From the above one can see the complexity, compared with just buying a can of paint as one used to many years ago. Modern systems have to satisfy many parameters such as durability in service, cost effectiveness per unit degree of gloss, resistance to attack (from fuels, industrial fall outs and stone-chipping, for example) and for the amateur refinisher or home sprayer, the easiest system may not necessarily be the best, so there will always have to be a compromise. After all not many people have a spray oven in their garage or workshop!

The table below gives the most durable and resistant finishes in decreasing order. It follows that the last is the easiest to apply for the DIY refinisher.

High bake paints (TSA, TPA, enamels)	major car manufacturers only
Low bake enamels	requires expensive oven equipment. Major bodyshops
Two-pack acrylic	requires external (clean air) breathing source—used in large bodyshops
Air dry synthetic enamels with or without hardener	ideal for all refinishers
Acrylic enamels—base coat and clear systems	as above
Cellulose	major re-finish technique for all small operators
Brushing cellulose	virtually obsolete, for home use only

As with paint systems the **primers** are varied and it is vitally important to use the correct ones compatible with the paint scheme. Primers are used to provide a good key between the existing paint surface and the new one to be applied, and initially to cover new or bare patches of metal or GRP. Primers in use are as follows :-

1   Etch primer. This is a conventional primer, but it contains phosphoric acid, which etches into the surface. Used on new metal. Essential to use etch primers on aluminium panels.
2   Cellulose or synthetic primer. Ordinary primer, normally 2 coats are applied. Should never be flatted down, only de-nibbed. These are not designed to fill scratches and score marks.
3   'Hi-build' primers, e.g. International 'Superfil'. As above, but contain more pigments and are used to fill minor sanding marks. Each coat gives a thicker layer than a normal primer. Two or three coats are sprayed. These are flatted with 600 wet and dry sand paper to give a perfect surface. The film must be broken otherwise a further recoating is necessary.
4   Spray fillers (ICI polyester spray filler). These are **not** the same as hi-build primers. They are a resin/chalk mix which is mixed with a hardener and then sprayed on. Each coat gives up to 9 thou (0.009 in.) thickness. Used extensively on new GRP bodies and on GRP repairs. Flatted off with 220 wet and dry paper and must be overcoated with conventional primers. Will

Mixing the spray filler with the hardener. About an hour's working time, it is essential to clean out the gun with the solvent (acetone) before it goes off

Above **Spray filler being applied to this Elan after a front section has been put on. Note the masking on the waist line behind the wheel arch; this is because the Elan was duotone yellow and white; the white section was undamaged and did not require painting. The masking tape was taken along the Sprint decal line**

Left **Spray filler being used on this stripped MGC alloy bonnet. The filler has etch properties, but even so the bonnet was well keyed. It is essential to use the correct etch primers on bare aluminium. Note the unpainted Elan behind**

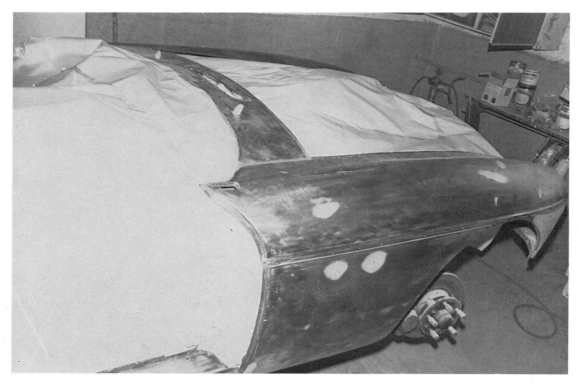

A sequence showing the use of cellulose (or polyester) stopper. The front wing of this MGB has been repaired locally using filler (P 38) then two coats of hi-build primer. Slight blemishes remaining (e.g. pinholes) were stoppered up in thin layers. The rear wing required more extensive treatment with stopper. Spray filler should have been used on the rear wing, indeed on the whole car as it was stripped back to bare metal, but as it takes longer to do (hence more money) than with conventional primer and stopper, the owner of this MGB did not wish to pay the extra. The problem is that this acreage of stopper may give problems later on (blistering). The stopper is flatted off with 600 paper then the whole body overcoated with primer, which is de-nibbed prior to colour

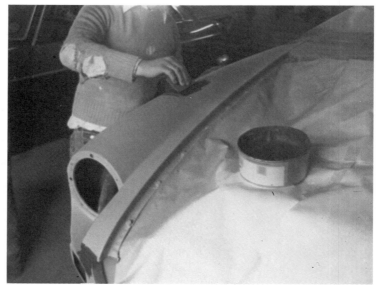

cover up to 80 grade sand paper marks. Has slight etching properties. This product has revolutionised GRP spraying. Must be sprayed while using an external (clean air) air supply.

5   Non-sand primers. Primers that require no flatting or de-nibbing, for top coats are sprayed directly onto its surface. **Not** recommended for the small or home operator, but used in commercial bodyshops for minimum turn round time.

6   Chip-resistant primers contain more plasticisers in them to help resist stone chips, and are ideally used on front, rear panels and sills. Can be overpainted with the body colour.

Specialist paints such as Finnigans Hammerite can also be used on sills to very good effect.

Thinners (solvents) come in many formulations and their correct use cannot be over-stressed. Cheap thinners will ruin many resprays and it is essential to use the same make of the thinners as it is for the paint. Thinners come in a range of applications, for example; cellulose, the range is as follows—Slow (International No. 35) for hot weather, Non-Bloom which can be used in adverse damp conditions, Fast (No. 86) for normal application, and Part Repair (No. 88) for what it says, just that.

There are different synthetic thinners as well, some used for air-drying, and others for low bake schedules. Spray fillers use acetone as their solvent.

Stoppers (knifing stoppers, or putties). These are heavily pigmented putties, used to fill deep score and scratch marks, and pin-holes in fillers. Applied by plastic spreader or broad knife, in thin layers. All the solvent must evaporate before overcoating. On most GRP bodies, spray filler alleviates the need for stoppers. Stoppers can be obtained for spray application. Stoppers come in two forms, nitrocellulose and two pack polyester, the latter hardens by chemical means and drying in between coats will not present a problem. This is used on synthetic systems, and on GRP bodies. After drying, the stopper is flatted with 600 wet and dry paper—used wet—and must be primered.

Stopper being used locally on this boot lid. The area around the hole has been flatted off but the other has been left in the applied state for comparison

Sealers and isolators

These are used to prevent the old paint surface from wrinkling up, or bleeding through the new finish. Many are available, and most use methyl alcohol as the solvent. Many extravagant claims are made for them and most of them simply do *not* work. Nothing will hold back more than two or three coats of paint, and the only answer on any vehicle for a lasting finish, is to strip it all off and start again. Sealers will *not* hold back flaky paintwork, nor will some of them allow the mixing of different paint systems. Synthetic can be sprayed on cellulose, but not the other way round. All sealers/isolators must not be flatted, and *must* be overcoated with primer before flatting takes place.

I have had many paint representatives visit me to try and impress me with their superb new sealer—'just the thing for fibreglass'. All failed after I sprayed them on a 21 year old Lotus Elite, and watched the paint surface pickle up. Undoubtedly sealers do work and I have used some excellent ones (and still do when respraying over ten year old vehicles) but their limitations *must* be realised. They cannot be expected to deal with multi-layers of old paint. I will name the ones that I have used and which are excellent—they are International, ICI, Parsons, Valentine and Glasurit.

Always seek advice first on the use of sealers.

Chapter 2 | Basic equipment and techniques

There are many basic items which have to be collected, or bought, before any repair and painting can begin. Metal and GRP bodies both share the same repair materials, with the exception of welding equipment and lead or braze filling. To undertake any part repair or full respray you will require most of the following:

Sandpapers: Production paper is chips of carborundum glued to a backing paper, used dry, varying in grades from P40 (very coarse) to P800 (very fine). Normally P80 is used for rubbing down fillers.

Wet and dry; made of silica chips on a waterproof backing paper in grades from 40 up to 1500. Used for all wet flatting applications. Most commonly used are 80 grade for coarse flatting of fillers and metal, 220 for spray fillers, 320 (or 360) and 600 for flatting bodies prior to painting, 800 for de-nibbing primers, and finally 1200 for flatting in between colour coats and the final colour coat prior to compounding.

With the sandpapers go cork and rubber blocks to provide an even pressure when sanding down. Rubber blocks (3M make a good one) are always used for wet and dry as cork will break up if used continuously with water. The specialist production files are invaluable, 3M making a good range. Special boxes of production paper are used with one tacky side so that it is held firmly on the file. When the paper is exhausted just peel it off and stick another strip on. Well worth buying if doing a large area rubbing down of filler. P80 is the most versatile paper.

Fillers, GRP materials; resin and mat for the repair of

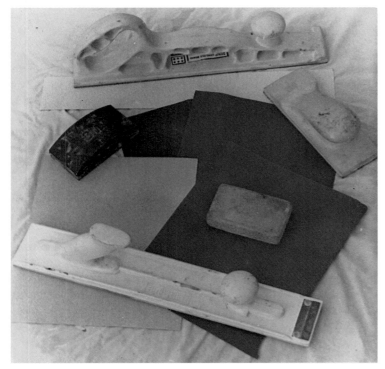

Above **A combined air filtration and warm air blower unit. This unit keeps the air free of particles and gives a good circulation of warm air. It should be standard equipment in all professional bodyshops**

Left **Essential equipment in the shape of sandpapers, rubber and cork blocks and production paper files**

Tak rags are inexpensive and are essential for all painting work; they are cloth rags impregnated with a sticky adhesive which gathers up all the dirt or sandings on the surface

GRP bodies and also to some metal bodied ones. P40, made by David's, is invaluable—this is chopped strand mat and resin mixed in a paste, which sets by the addition of hardener. Used for all applications. Fillers are basically chalk dust and resin mixed to a creamy paste, and set with the aid of a hardener. Many are available but David's P38, and U-pol C are excellent.

Masking tape: absolutely essential for the correct covering of all parts left on the car that are not to be painted. Always buy the proper tape, but do *not* use Sellotape or insulating tape. Masking tape comes in sizes from 0.5 in. (13 mm) wide up to 3 in. (75 mm). 1 in. (25 mm) is the most versatile with 2 in (50 mm) used for bumpers, and other long flat items. Approximately two rolls of 1 in will be needed for one complete respray. Most people mask with newspaper but this is technically incorrect, as the thinners in the overspray may bleed out the printing ink in the paper and cause staining on the bodywork. **Never** use colour magazines. There are available proper masking tape and brown paper dispensing stands, that automatically put the tape on one edge of the paper when pulled; very useful for high volume paint operators but hardly suitable for the 'one off' job.

Masking up technique is simple, but care and attention must be paid to awkward corners and crevices. Start by removing all the components that can be removed, as this will take about the same time as trying to mask them up, then mask up from the top downwards, starting with all the glass area. Go around the rubber seal first with tape only, then offer up two sheets of newspaper (one is not sufficient thickness) and tape to the first tape. Mask up any overlapping sheets as it is surprising where spray drift gets to. Cover the window frames, and lights in this manner. Use several strips of 2 in. wide tape for the bumpers. If radio or CB aerials cannot be removed, mask up the aerial vertically with one piece wrapped round and the two ends stuck together; this way makes for easy removal rather than by masking up in a spiral. If windscreens are removed or the doors are off the car, remove all the seals. Mask on the

Using two inch wide tape to mask up a bumper

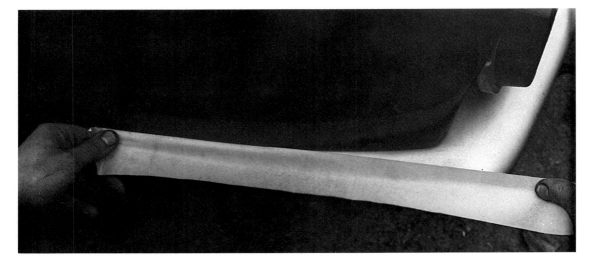

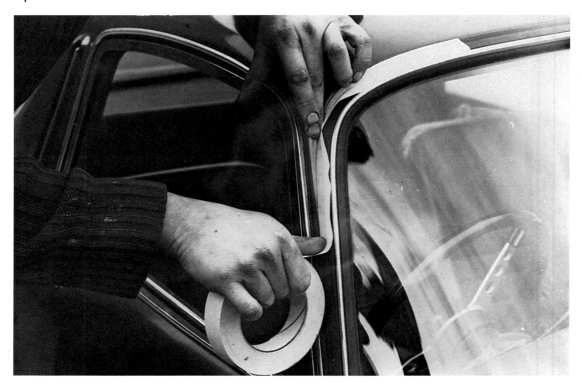

A sequence showing the masking up of a windscreen. First run a line of tape, then use the flat screen surface to tape up the paper, press on to the first, then press well down. Mask up all overlapping sheets to prevent overspray finding its way onto the glass and tearing off with the spray pressure

Left **Masking up the aerial vertically, which is easier to undo than masking done up in a spiral**

Above **Masking up inside the lip
to ensure that all the flange is
painted. Note the stopper on the
side panel**

Right **The original colour
underneath. You *must* remove all
stickers before re-painting. It
would have taken longer to mask
up this sticker than it would to
remove it**

outside edge of the lip to a depth of $\frac{3}{8}$ in. (10 mm), for after removal the seals will hide the line, or mask internally by taping on the inside, then sticking the paper on the outside to the exposed sticky edge. In this way all the lip will be painted and if a change of colour is being made nobody will know. All too often, by removing trims on an older car one can see all the different colours that have gone before. I can never understand why people do not remove parts that can be removed, for to see spray drift on door seals and the like is really to see poor workmanship. There can be no excuse for it.

Make sure that all the tape is stuck down well, as it has to survive countless soakings in water, blowing off with compressed air, and finally the bombardment of paint. If the tape starts to lift or peel off, at any stage, remove and re-do the section. Remove the tape and paper as soon as the paint is completely dry (with some synthetic enamels, peel them off before the paint is dry—when the paint is still tacky—because if solidly dry the plastic film will tear or come off with the tape, leaving an awful mess). If any

Bad masking up on a windscreen rubber, showing the overspray

Again attention to detail. Overspray on the filler neck grommet which has cracked away due to vibration and rough handling with the pump fuel nozzle. It only takes a few minutes to remove the cap and filler neck and then refit a new grommet after painting

tape remains, roll it up with your finger, or very carefully scrape off using a blunt flat blade or—if well and truly stuck (if it has been left masked up for weeks)—very carefully moisten it in petrol to dissolve the adhesive. Do *not* use thinners, or allow the fuel to come into contact with the new paint. This method can also be used for caked-on aged tape.

Masks: These are essential for any painting work. The simplest type is the metal face piece that presses a renewable multi-layered cotton pad to your nose and mouth. One type is the Martingdale available at chemists and most home centres. This is cheapest, but is not really suited for paint spraying as the layers fill up too quickly. Equal to the cotton layer type is the metal frame type that fits like a cup over the nose and mouth. The wire frame is interwoven in a gauze material that provides the filter. Ideal for limited spray use in the open air, but inside the same limitations apply as with the cotton type. Both these types are not cumbersome to use and are best suited for protection against filler dust when sanding down repairs.

Perhaps the most versatile type that is used in most paint shops is the rubber mask that has an integral renewable charcoal filter. It looks like a modern version of a wartime gas mask. This type is essential when spraying at home or in a confined space. They are relatively inexpensive to buy, and they can be hired along with your spray equipment.

The final type is the helmet variety that has its own self-

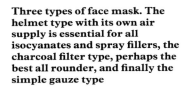

Three types of face mask. The helmet type with its own air supply is essential for all isocyanates and spray fillers, the charcoal filter type, perhaps the best all rounder, and finally the simple gauze type

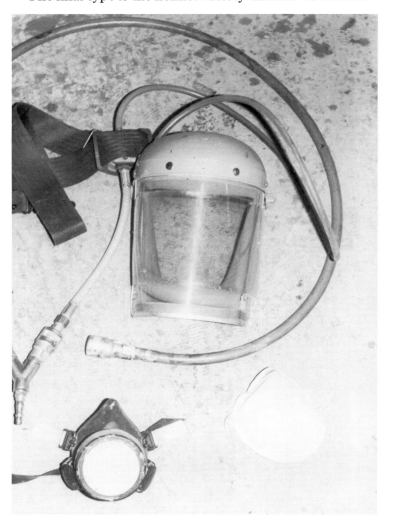

The air control is at the back, and the fluid control on the side of this Widar spray gun

contained outside air supply. It is really the only type to use when applying all paint. Essential for isocyanate type paints and spray fillers (see Health and Safety chapter). Costly to buy, and only in use in professional body shops.

Make sure your clothing is suitable as well. Wear reasonably tight fitting shirts or sweaters, otherwise when leaning over the car a dangling shirt sleeve or loose sweater may ruin the paint finish. Never wear hobnailed boots or shoes, as if you slip, an errant spark may flash off the heavy thinner vapour.

Other tools needed will be a selection of rasp files, drills, grinderette or cintride disc on an electric drill, welding equipment, zintex sheets (for making new panels or part repair of an old panel), rust preventers and other details. (The repairs of both GRP and metal-bodied cars are covered in other books in this series.)

Spray equipment: There is no substitute for a professional spray finish, and by that I mean using a compressed air spray gun and a proper compressor. Some of the other appliances give the same degree of finish as would a 10 in. wallpaper brush. Paint spraying is a skilled operation which takes many years to perfect and for the first time painter there is no possible way he can hope to achieve the results of someone with five or more years experience. However, the choice of equipment and technique is all important to help him on his way.

Many types of spray equipment are available and I can only advise that you ask your local paint supplier to the trade, or your nearest professional spray shop, as to what type would be ideally suited to your particular needs. An entire book could be written about spray guns and technique alone, but as a guide I hope the following will be of use: Do not buy or hire an electric spray gun, which are airless guns driven by an electric motor. They may be ideal for spraying heavier materials (such as varnish on a flat wood panel) but they are totally useless for spraying a car. The finish is awful, and hours and hours of polishing work will have to take place. I am not dismissing these out of hand for I've used one (Burgess), which was very good to my particular application, of painting an inside of a boat.

Although messy on the outside, it is absolutely spotless on the inside

Another type that is often advertised for the home sprayer is the constant pressure type, a self contained package that has a motor driving a compressor but with no holding tank, so that a permanent set pressure is at the gun. This is called a constant bleed gun. It is relatively useful for the one-off job, fairly cheap to buy but very noisy as the motor is running permanently. Useful too for having a compressed air supply for other jobs as well. Reasonable results can be achieved with this.

The 'normal' type is the proper compressor arrangement supplying air to the gun. Small units have an electric motor driving a compressor which supplies compressed air to a holding tank. Large units may have an external holding tank. Small units can be wheeled about on their own wheels. The unit of measure is cfm which stands for cubic feet per minute and a compressor rating of 3 cfm means that the tank will hold a constant rating of three cubic feet a minute. If buying or hiring a compressor it is essential that you obtain one of the correct rating. One of 4.5 cfm will be sufficient for a respray. With a smaller capacity the supply of air will not keep up with the demand of the gun, and you'll always be waiting for the compressor to catch up, and the results will suffer.

If hiring a unit, make sure that it will hold air; if the motor permanently cuts in and air is leaking out of all the seals take it back, because in this application you cannot afford to wait while the pressure builds up. All compressors have a safety blow off valve fitted; make sure that a regulator is fitted as well, as you want to know what pressure you're spraying at (usually between 45–60 psi). In any case the compressor will shut off at anywhere between 120–200 psi.

If buying a compressor be guided by your local factor. Air lines and fittings must be of the correct type. A length of garden hose and jubilee clips will not do!

Spray guns vary enormously; be guided by your local factor. Prices vary a lot; unless you are going to spray many vehicles, then the top of the range type (say, De Vilbiss) will not be necessary as a good medium price gun will suffice. Some cheap ones are really only good for primers, chassis blacks or even for spraying Waxoyl and Ham-

merite. Be guided also regarding the gun jet sizes. State clearly what paint system you intend to use (cellulose, synthetic, spray fillers or whatever) and, hopefully, you should be given the correct jet for the gun. Most guns are, of course, ready to use straight away, with the basic settings.

Spray technique. It is essential to do it right, in order to achieve the good finish.

1   Air pressure must be correct—usually 45–60 psi.
2   Paint viscosity must be correct. On all paint information sheets and cans you will see the legend: 21–24 sec. on BS cup B4 at 20 degrees C—this means that for a given amount of thinned paint passing through an aperture (British Standard viscosity cup B4) at room temperature, between 21–24 sec. will be needed. Not many people care about this and just thin down to 50/50, if cellulose. However, if you do it correctly, a uniform paint specification will always be in the spray gun.
3   Stir the paint well, especially if it has been mixed and is not an 'off the shelf' stock colour. Always try to buy in larger $2\frac{1}{2}$ or 5 litre cans, rather than one litre cans, as these may vary slightly in colour if they have been specially mixed.
4   Experiment first to get the spray pattern right. Pin a clean piece of paper to a wall, and adjust the volume and air controls on the gun until a perfect spray pattern is achieved.
5   When spraying, the gun should be held at right angles to the surface, 6–9 in. away from it. It must be moved at a uniform speed and at a uniform distance. **Never** swing the gun in an arc,

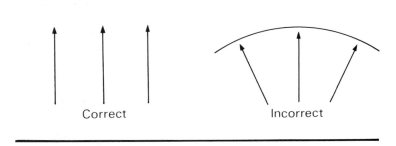

Correct   Incorrect

Damping down prior to spraying. Just enough water is sprinkled on the floor to prevent any dust flying up onto the vehicle when the gun is in action. Do not soak the floor otherwise moisture droplets may affect the final paint surface. The MGB rear wing has just had a single coat of primer on it after a minor repair—Note the well feathered primer/original paint edge prior to priming the whole body

as the paint will then be thicker in the middle, than on the edges. The wrist must not flex.

Above **A sequence demonstrating the handling of a spray gun, and the correct distance from the panel**

Right **Too close—would give runs and sags**

Top opposite **Too far away— would give a dry spray**

Bottom opposite **Not held at right angles to the surface. Will give uneven spray pattern**

The gun must be held in line with the wrist and forearm

Always overlap the previous strike by at least 50 per cent to achieve correct covering.

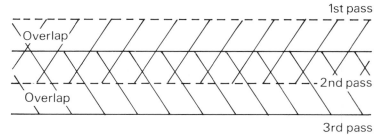

Stick to a standard spray system, starting on the roof and working around the car in a clockwise direction, i.e.:

Do not allow the wrist to twist and flex

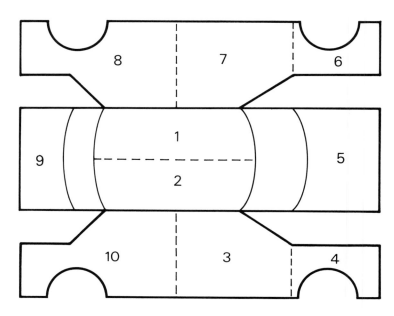

1 **N/S roof**
2 **O/S roof**
3 **O/S door**
4 **O/S/F wing**
5 **bonnet**
6 **N/S/F wing**
7 **N/S door**
8 **N/S/R wing**
9 **Boot lid**
10 **O/S/R wing**

Use the same sequence on spraying the shell, even if the doors, bonnet and boot lid are off the car.

Always spray the door shuts, bonnet lips, boot lips and under-side of bonnets and boot lids first. Do the 'exterior' of the car last.

6 Always allow sufficient time in between coat applications (flash off time) otherwise heavy wet build up will lead to all sorts of troubles.

7 Clean the spray gun thoroughly after use. It must be spotless, otherwise any hardened paint left inside will come out the next time you use it and ruin the new finish, especially if it's a different colour. All the jets must be absolutely clear otherwise an erratic spray pattern will result the next time round. A can of cheaper thinners can be bought for cleaning out equipment.

If you have bought your own compressor remember to drain out the water of the holding tank or from the water trap—compressed air is hot, and on cooling, moisture is created. Maintain the unit in accordance with the manufacturer's instructions.

Chapter 3 | **Health and safety**

The importance of looking after oneself whilst working with paint materials cannot be stressed too highly. Paints and thinners are highly volatile substances and can cause serious fires if exposed to naked flames. The flash points of most paints are between 22–32 degrees C but some have a flash point below 22 degrees C (74 degrees F). The following precautions must be observed :-

a.   Buy a sufficient quantity for the job in hand, (this includes resins if required as well) and store in a cool place away from excessive heat, such as direct sunlight. Failure to do this can result in heat build-up inside the cans, which will in turn vaporise the thinner content and the resultant pressure will blow the lid off. Apart from the awful mess which results anyone standing near can get hurt. After use, always replace the lids or caps firmly. Dispose of the empty cans safely, **do not** throw them on the fire, as the cans will explode because of the vapour content inside.

If any paint is left over, this can be kept for touch-up purposes. However, as with resins, they have a 'shelf-life'; after 12–18 months they must be thrown away. Paint will deteriorate, along with some thinners and hardeners, if kept for a longer period than this.

With all paints and thinners it is an offence to pour any residues down the drains, and severe penalties can be expected if you are caught. All residues spilt must be soaked up in sand or earth, and then buried.

b.   Ensure good ventilation and air movement, as the vapour build up is tremendous. Make sure there are no naked flames, **do not smoke, do wear rubber soled shoes or boots** to eliminate sparks from 'hob-nailed' boots, **do not use open radiant fires or Calor gas type heaters** to heat up the painting area, for if they are left on whilst spraying, the flash point will be exceeded and devastation will result. Hire a correct heater, and achieve an overall warmth before spraying; spray, then heat again. Make sure that no electrical wires are live and dangling to cause a spark. Do not have extra lead lines to plug in extra lighting. It is better to rig up two or four flourescent tubes from a wall socket to achieve an overall degree of good light. If there are any electrical appliances that you do not require, take them out of the painting area. Always have a dry powder type fire extinguisher to hand.

c.   When painting always **wear a mask**—preferably the type with the disposable air filter.

Under no circumstances spray iso-cyanates without an external air source. Leave this to the professional, if you require this type of paint scheme. In brief, in this process cyanide vapour is produced and is **lethal** if breathed in even for a short period. The same applies

This Morris Traveller has just been primered. The photograph is intended to show the high vapour build up in the surrounding atmosphere. In a small garage the car would almost be invisible

to the polyester spray fillers. (Do outside or brush apply—
see later on).

Any rags soaked in thinners or paint after painting must
be thrown away carefully, or burnt under supervision. If
burning them, do not pile on all at once and light up as
the resultant flash back may burn your arms and face
severely.

d.   If accidents do happen, try not to panic and try to act
logically.

Spillage: even when opening a new can cover with a rag,
prise off the lid gently, to release any pressure build up.
If you have them, wear protective goggles. Mop up as
described.

Fire: if this is small, extinguish with the extinguisher
(BCF type) or smother with sand. Do not use water, as
this will spread the fire. Paints and thinners do not mix
with water.

If you cannot contain the fire, then immediately
telephone the fire brigade, otherwise serious building
damage will occur and the vehicle will be lost as well. Apart
from the obvious loss, prosecution may follow from the
local council, as spraying is usually strictly forbidden. The
householders' insurance policy will refuse to pay on any
claim, and the vehicle insurance company will not pay up
either (if it is insured in the first place).

Think before you spray at home, for one tiny mistake
could end in total disaster. Fire is the major cause of
damage whilst spraying in the garage.

Personal health: if any paint or thinners comes into contact with your eyes, wash them under running water for
at least ten minutes. If irritation persists, medical attention
must be sought immediately.

Even if you wear a mask, if drowsiness or dizziness
occurs because of over exposure to the paint vapour, get
out immediately into the fresh air and keep warm. Your
health is more important than finishing the panel. If you
still feel unwell when returning to the job even with proper
ventilation, then you may be allergic to the chemicals or
smell. **Do not continue**—let someone else or a professional finish the job. People with asthma or bronchial
infections should **not** spray. If you persist while feeling

dizzy, you may find that eventually the high vapour saturation will starve the air of oxygen, and you will become unconscious.

If any paint or thinners are swallowed, then drink copious amounts of water. **Do not induce vomiting** as lung damage may result by the inhaling of the thinner content (especially cellulose paints, 50–50 mixed with thinner). Medical attention must be sought immediately. If there is any spillage on the skin, wash it off with soap and water, and use a cream (Nivea etc.). Before starting use a barrier cream and rub well in.

It is not advisable to wash the paint off with thinners, as constant washing can give rise to dermatitis.

All the above is frightening to read, but sadly these accidents do happen every year by people being very careless and slap happy ('I've sprayed before in my garage—no problems . . .'). I have to state the precautions and preventions you should follow—and every paint manufacturer prints the dangers on their cans. Please follow them; there is no reason why your task cannot be achieved in perfect safety.

Chapter 4 | What can and does go wrong

Here are some guide lines to help you rectify any disasters.

1   Air pressure too high may give rise to:

a. A dry spray
b. Loss of gloss
c. Orange peel finish

too little paint atomising before it hits the surface

Air pressure too low may provoke:

a. Runs
b. Pinholing
c. Solvent popping

too heavy a paint build up

2a.   Spray gun held too close will give the same effect as low air pressure, and if held too far away the effect will be the same as having too high an air pressure.

b.   If the fluid nozzle is set too high with a low capacity air cap this will give rise to paint runs, and vice versa too low a fluid nozzle and high air cap, will result in a dry spray.

c.   Spray pattern wrong (i.e. fan width too narrow): will give rise to striping noticeable on metallics, dark and light streaks. In addition, not holding the gun at right angles to the surface will also give rise to striping.

Spraying metallics requires a little more concentration on technique, but it is not as difficult as people make out. Some excellent first time results have been achieved by people who pay attention to detail as regards fan patterns. Always remember to keep the paint in the gun well agitated in between passes. Stir the paint well in the beginning.

3   Defects that can happen during and after paint application:

Dirt

Bits of muck being trapped on the paint surface. This is *the* major source of problems for the home sprayer.

If dirt is resting on the surface wait until this has hardened completely then wet flat with 1200 paper and soap. Compound, T-cut and wax.

Make sure the workshop is well swept before starting, and well dampened down. Rafters and ceilings must be spotless, especially if you are using an air dry synthetic, as the heavy vapour will literally pull down dirt from the top as the vapour settles.

All clothes should be clean, and all muck should be blown out of the crevices on the car, from gutters, channels and door shuts. Any left over will soon be blasted onto the paint surface at 60 psi.

Make sure the compressor has a clean air filter on it. If not, clean it or replace it. Dirty air can cause contamination.

Make sure all equipment is spotlessly clean.

If dirt has been sprayed over then the area will have to be flattened off completely, and re-sprayed again.

Runs, dribbles, sags

The second most major problem, mainly due to inexperience. They occur on awkward corners, or on a flat vertical surface such as door. Make sure the spraying technique is correct. Don't hold the gun too close, move with a uniform speed, get correct air pressure and viscosity of paint. Use the correct grade of thinners.

Make sure of good ventilation and air movement and warmth. Allow the correct flash off time in between coats, and don't pile it on all at once.

With all runs and sags, allow them to harden off completely. With synthetic enamels this may take weeks, then wet flat with 1200 paper and soap, which will take a long time. Compound, T-cut and wax. If this is not satisfactory, then wet flat with 600 paper and re-spray the area again.

With synthetic, if the sag is still soft after the initial flat with 1200 paper, wait until that has hardened off and continue.

More often than not, a synthetic 'sag' means the whole panel has to be re-done.

Bubbles (known as **blowing**. This is not the same as **blistering**)

Air bubbles trapped under the paint film.

Due to poor filling technique, allowing air to be trapped.

Happens more frequently on GRP bodies than metal, but any repair using fillers, stoppers, solders, and mastics must be done correctly.

On all repairs, make sure the edges are feathered out properly, and never leave a sharp edge. On metal cars, make sure that all new seams have no trapped air pockets. Air bubbles will appear during a low bake or force drying, also during the hot summer (as the air expands). They disappear in winter, as opposed to blistering which appears in damp weather and disappears in hot!

On metal cars strip off all paint to the surface, or repair and start again.

On GRP cars treat as a gel-crack and grind the affected area, resin, tissue and filler and then repaint.

Unlike blisters that are on the top surface, trapped air bubbles are on the substrata, and the only feasible rectification is to start again.

Bleeding

Occurs when the old pigment dissolves into the thinners of the newly applied paint. Reds, yellows and maroons are most susceptible to this. Make sure that paint equipment is spotless. Always test a piece first where it doesn't show. It is not advisable to spray white or light colours over red and maroon.

If any bleeding occurs through the primers, then lightly de-nib with 800 paper and spray with a coat of bleeding inhibitor sealer, then re-prime and colour. If it still bleeds through, then strip off all the paint back to bare GRP or metal and repaint in the colour of your choice.

Blushing (often mistakenly called **blooming**)

The paint goes milky on the surface. Due almost entirely to damp spraying conditions.

With slight milkiness a good compounding, T-cut and wax should restore the colour and gloss.

Make sure all surfaces are dry and the spray area is adequately heated. Good air movement is essential as well. If it is a really dull, foggy damp day, do not spray, but wait until conditions improve, because as soon as the heat is turned off, damp will be drawn onto the paint surface.

If severe, then flat off with 600 paper, wet, and re-paint.

Make sure of correct use of thinners. If doing a part repair in adverse conditions then **non-bloom** thinners are available. Not recommended for full resprays.

Craters, Fish-eyes, Saucers (all known professionally as **Cissing**)

Paint surface has craters on it varying in size and depth.

The only rectification is to wet flat down to a solid base, until all the craters have gone, then re-paint.

The cause is purely due to contamination by waxes, silicone based compounds, oils, grease, soaps or detergents. Make sure the paint surface is grease-free by using a solvent wipe (white spirit) and a tak rag. Make sure all traces of underbody sealants (Ziebart, Dinitrol, Waxoyl etc.) are removed from the surrounding paint area—for these all contain silicones. On part repairs, make sure that no wax remains where overspray is likely to occur. De-wax with white spirit. Check that compressor seals are not leaking and allowing oil mist into the holding tank. Air lines must be of the correct type.

Dry spray and cobwebbing

Cobwebbing is a situation where the paint arrives on the surface in filaments (rather like GRP mat); it has failed to atomise. As with dry spray make sure paint is not cold or too thick—get the viscosity right and the air pressure as well.

Dry spray is the opposite of runs and sags i.e. the paint hits the surface in a dry, powdery state, due to poor spraying technique. The gun is held too far away and moved across the surface too quickly, or the air pressure set too high. Sometimes due to wrong use of thinners (i.e. too fast a thinner on a hot day).

Make sure spray gun is set up correctly.

Cobwebbing—allow to harden off, wet flat with 600 paper, then 800, and re-paint. Dry spray—if sound on the top coat may be wet flatted with 1200 paper and soap, compounded, T-cut and waxed to restore the gloss.

If not confined to the top coat, then wet flat colour and primer coats to a sound base and re-paint.

Dry spray metallic coat has to be wet flatted and re-painted. If left, metallic particles will oxidise giving a flat dull surface.

Dry spray. Very bobbly surface. Flatting and polishing would restore the surface and gloss

Cracking, crazing, splitting

The paint surface literally crazes, either during the application or even starting to appear some years later.

On initial application, the causes are incorrect use of paint systems. Never sandwich synthetic type finishes between cellulose, always keep to one scheme throughout, and that applies to stoppers as well. Never mix paint schemes from different manufacturers.

If repainting over clear lacquer it is essential to wet flat all the layers off back to solid colour.

Any crazing must be removed completely. A true clear lacquer does not last, and at Fibreglass Services we add up to 20 per cent lacquer to the final colour coats when spraying metallics. This is for cellulose metallics; the acrylic base coat and clear needs a different system. By doing this method all yellowing and crazing will be eliminated.

An extreme case of cracking and flaking off. A strip back to bare GRP or metal would be required here, and one should start again. The Ford colours, blue mink and silver fox gave problems on the Mk 2 Cortinas similar to this, and Ford repainted many of them again

Another cause is overcoating synthetic enamels before the original enamel has thoroughly dried (cured), or waiting too long in between first and second coats when respraying, so that the first layer has started to cure.

Overcoating of old lacquer surfaces may also give rise to crazing. After application, in a few months or years time the lacquer surface will start to craze. This is due to too many layers of clear lacquer being added over the final top coat. The lacquer will degrade with the weather causing yellowing and crazing. Keep lacquer coats to a minimum.

Alternatively one thin layer on a top coat will have the same effect. Some sealer coats may react with a newly painted surface.

'Pure' cracking as opposed to crazing can be caused by too thick a paint build up—excessive total paint thickness after many successive resprays is too great for any more to 'take' and the paint cracks with body flexing.

If paint thickness is too great all must be stripped off, back to bare GRP or metal. After about four resprays strip off in any case.

On GRP bodies, painting directly over gel cracks and accident damage—the paint sinks into the cracks and as soon as the crack flexes the paint film is broken. On GRP and metal bodies, paint may crack over poor repairs.

Repairs must be carried out correctly before re-painting. Painting over cracks serves no purpose whatsoever.

Popping—air bubbles trapped in the paint film

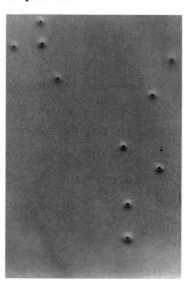

Pinholing, popping (see also blowing)

Literally this means bubbles with a pin-hole in them on the surface, and is caused by too rapid drying of the paint surface, trapping air underneath.

If limited to the last few coats both may be eliminated by flatting with 1200 paper and soap, then compound, T-cut and wax.

Spray conditions must be correct. Too high an ambient temperature with too rapid an air movement will cause popping, also too high a viscosity and too low an air pressure as well. Spraying heavy colour coats over a dry spray primer will trap air in the 'bobbly' primer surface.

If not, then they must be flatted out completely with 600 paper, wet, then the panel re-painted.

One must not overspray the pinholes as this will not work, and in fact it accentuates the defect.

Incorrect use of thinners.
Make sure all filler on repairs
is covered by primers, colour
sprayed straight on to filler
will result in pin holing (and
loss of gloss). If any pinholes
are in the original paint
surface these must be
removed completely (see also
blistering) otherwise they will
come through the new layers.

Poor bonding or adhesion peeling

Newly applied paint surface
peels off with masking tape or
chips off when on the road, up
to many months afterwards.
The chip edges may lift and
can be peeled back.

This is caused by poor
bonding of primer or colour
coats to its preceding layer.

Make sure surfaces are not
contaminated by oils, greases,

The only rectification is to wet
flat or strip the paint back to a
sound base and re-paint again.

Failure to do this will result in
the paint just peeling and
peeling away until all the
'colour' has gone.

If just confined to bad
masking technique then wet
flat and feather the edges well,
and repaint.

Below right **The familiar rust
bubbles pushing the paint film up
from underneath. Even after
short term repairs a new wing
will eventually be needed**

Below **Poor adhesion here
between the final coat and
undercoats. Paint actually peels
off in strips**

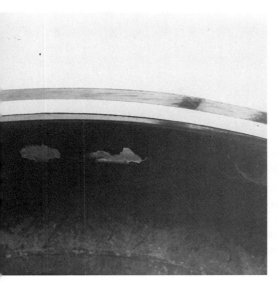

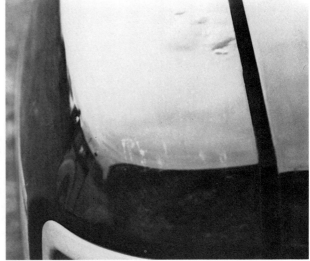

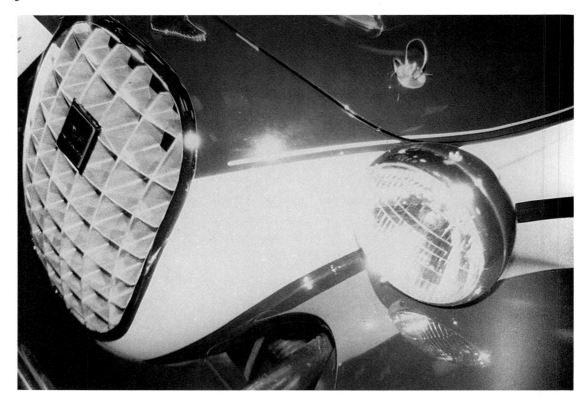

A duotone scheme with painted waistline. Great care is needed here in masking up, if any local blow-ins have to be tackled

detergents, or dirt (see cissing and dirt).

Never mix paint manufacturers schemes— always go throughout with an International, ICI, Glasurit or other system. Make sure that thinners are correct and not mixed. Use correct primers for GRP, aluminium, and steel.

Make sure on two colour panels that the first is thoroughly dry before masking up to paint the second.

Orange peel and lined (scratched) surface

Two other defects common to the first time sprayer. A 'flat' finish is a perfectly flat smooth mirror like finish whereas orange peel is a finish that resembles the skin of an orange. (If very bad, it is unkindly referred to as a Braille finish!).

All new mass production cars have a slight orange peel effect, for this is common with all TPA and TSA and high bake enamel finishes. If care is taken over the refinishing of cellulose and acrylic systems then a flat finish is achieved.

Orange peel is caused by the same effects as for runs and sags.

Lined or scratched surface is caused by incorrect use of flatting paper. Too coarse a grade abrades a surface too much for the top coats to fill. Primers may not be fully dry before overcoating, or just the spraying of colour on the old colour with no primers in between.

Upon refinishing, make sure the surface is clean, otherwise a polishing mop or hand rubbing will pick up dirt and other muck and deeply score the surface.

Most orange peel and lines can be polished out when the surface is thoroughly dry. 1200 paper and soap may have to be used.

If too severe then a good wet flatting with 600 paper will be required, and a re-paint.

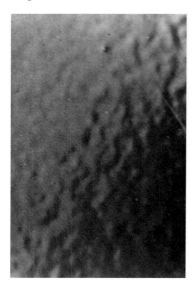

Very heavy orange peel. This is so bad that flatting and repainting would be the only recourse. Flatting and polishing would not help

It is essential to flat and feather correctly. Here, far too coarse a grade has been used and scratch opening will and has occurred here. Do not overcoat again but reflat back to a sound base using the correct grade of paper, and then re-paint

Sinkage

Paint dries off to show repairs and other defects.

This is most prevalent on GRP bodies due to bad repair technique, and not allowing sufficient time in between successive repair, primer or top coat applications. Sinkage can occur up to months afterwards as the paint finally hardens. All edges must be feathered out correctly, and no bare filler or stoppers must show through the primers. If using any isolators or sealers the surface of these must not be broken by flatting paper as the 'barrier' at that point will then be lost.

Too heavy an application on any one of the paint layers or too dry a layer (Porosity occurring especially in a primer layer) may also give rise to sinkage as can humid, cold, or damp drying conditions.

Sinkage will almost definitely occur when respraying on a high paint build up (i.e. after three or more previous sprays). The thinners will just lift the repair at the filler/paint boundary.

If slight, wait until sinkage stops i.e. when paint is fully hardened in two or three months, then wet flat with 1200 paper and soap, compound, T-cut and wax.

If severe, then the repair will have to be done again— *properly* this time (especially on GRP) and re-painted from the ground up.

If the repair will 'stand up', then a wet flat with 600 paper, and re-paint may hold back any further sinkage.

All paint should be stripped off and you should start again, paying particular attention to old repairs.

Wrinkling, puckering, shrivelling

The top paint surface wrinkles up upon drying. Caused by too heavy a build up of colour coats, and poor drying conditions. If too cold and humid with a high air movement, the top surface will be dried in the air stream, leaving the underneath still wet. Drying in a foul atmosphere will also produce wrinkling (also for loss of gloss as well). Make sure no exhaust or petrol fumes are being emitted near the spraying area.

Wait until thoroughly dry, then wet flat back to a sound base and repaint. Improve the drying conditions.

Blistering and micro blistering

Blistering, as opposed to bubbling, is the effect of moisture permeating through the paint film, and causing loss of adhesion between the base and paint film or between paint layers. All paints are permeable to water vapour, and this increases with age and especially on cellulose finishes over a period of time (usually after six to ten years). Minute blisters appear on the top surfaces—boot, roof, bonnet—these are known as micro blisters, and result in a loss of gloss. High and low bake enamels are water resistant, and no problem occurs. Air drying synthetics have a far greater resistance to water vapour than does cellulose.

With all blistering on a new surface the only correct rectification is to wet flat through to a sound base. If blistering has occurred from the spray filler hi-build primer layers, then all must be stripped back to bare metal or GRP again. Make sure all is thoroughly dry and repeat the respray, paying attention to the correct conditions.

Left **An horrific example of
wrinkling. The top surface dried
far too quickly (too high an air
movement or a foul atmosphere)
for the underneath to cope. A
strip back to bare GRP or metal
would be necessary here**

Below **Examples of micro-
blistering on these panels, due to
old age of the paint absorbing
moisture. A thorough flat and re-
paint is called for**

However, exposing any finish to permanently damp conditions before it has fully hardened, will almost certainly result in blisters. Air drying synthetics are more prone here than cellulose as they take at least two to three weeks to cure fully.

Storing a newly painted surface in a damp garage, with a cover over the vehicle for any length of time, will result in blisters forming.

Other causes are water contamination in the equipment perhaps because there is no water trap on the compressor, or the tank has not been drained, allowing water to enter the compressed air line and gun. Water retention on the surface: after all wet flatting of spray fillers and de-nibbing of primers the surface must be **bone dry** before applying colour coats.

Some spray fillers, putties and primers are notorious for holding water. Some act like brake fluid (hydroscopic), by absorbing moisture from the atmosphere. Lessanol is the worst offender; Lessanol is *not* a true spray filler and confusion arises between this and, say, ICI polyester spray filler, which is. Lessanol should be regarded as a high build stopper (primer). The spraying area should be brought well up to temperature before painting,

If micro-blistering occurs because of age, then a respray is well overdue.

If the vehicle has been painted a number of months, and blisters appear from damp storage conditions, a run out in the car on a dry sunny day will evaporate away the moisture. The vehicle must then be kept in a dry place, with good air circulation round it.

This is why blisters go away in summer and return in winter (as opposed to bubbling).

to allow any retained moisture to evaporate.

The use of cheap thinners can result in blistering and insufficient depth of paint— the film is too thin, allowing moisture to pass through more easily. Use of old paint (its chemical properties having changed) may have the same effect. Another blister which gives the same appearance as a moisture blister, is one containing solvent. This goes under the name of solvent trap, whereby the top surface film hardens off so rapidly that any underlying solvent will be trapped, only to try and escape through the film and cause the blister. These may be due to the operator, his technique and the drying conditions, but also to the type of paint system used.

Bronzing, chalking, colour separation

All three of these 'defects are really confined to old age of the paint film.

Bronzing occurs mainly on blue, black and maroon finishes, and occurs when these pigments are held loosely in a layer in the surface which differs slightly in colour from the other layers of pigments in the paint.

Chalking is the dry, dull powdery top film that comes off on your hand, caused by the degradation of the top

In all cases a good compound, T-cut and waxing will restore the gloss, though a respray will inevitably be necessary in due course.

Chalking has occurred here, due to old age of the paintwork. All gloss has gone and the top film is powdery to touch. Colour separation has taken place as well. A repaint is needed in this case

surface by sunlight and moisture. Lack of care is the main cause—for instance, cellulose finish which has not been polished for years, but just left to the elements.

Colour separation like the above is due to age. Different colour pigments go to make up a single solid colour, and these will degrade at varying speeds to give rise to colour changes. A sand colour may contain white, yellow and red pigments and in time these may 'settle' into light and darker pigmented patches.

Colour change may occur as a reaction from general traffic filth and from industrial fallouts (see a later chapter).

Colour change and bronzing may occur from new if the paint has not been mixed properly.

Traffic filth can be removed by T-cut and wax. More frequent car washing will be necessary to prevent build up again.

Poor covering (opacity)

Loss of gloss

Poor covering and loss of gloss are usually due to bad technique. Make sure the paint is properly stirred, the viscosity is right (over-thinned paint won't cover), and the air pressure not too high. Make sure to spray the correct number of coats (some colours have poor natural covering power anyway), and that drying conditions are correct.

If loss of gloss is slight, compound, T-cut and wax should restore. If not, wet flat with 800 paper and re-paint.

With poor opacity, allow to harden off, wet flat with 800 paper and re-coat correctly.

An example of poor covering. Pure yellow was brushed over black lettering, without any preparation

Having read through all that can happen you can see that many conditions overlap, and many defects are inter-related. But get the following things right, and much heart-ache should be avoided:

1   Thorough preparation and repair technique.
2   Correct spraying facilities and drying conditions.
3   Correct spray equipment and technique.
4   Correct paint scheme and application.
5   Correct refinishing of vehicle and storage conditions.

Poor spraying and finishing technique, overspray just left. Rectification is by flatting with 1200 paper, and soap and compound, T-Cut and wax

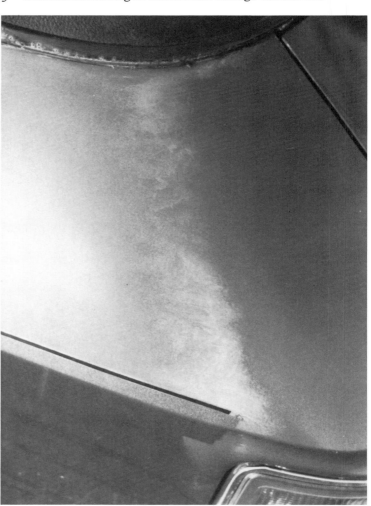

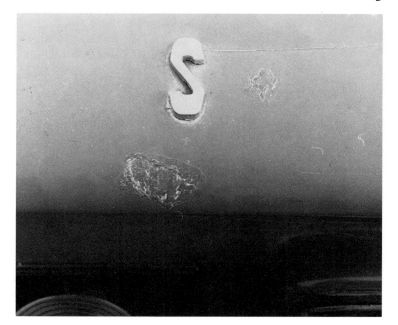

An example of slap-happy brush touch-up work. Care should be taken in confining the touch-up paint to the chip area, building up carefully after each 'dab' has fully dried. Finally one can flat off with 1200 paper and soap and polish, and you won't be able to see the difference. The white marks are dried wax trapped on the rough surface

Aerosols follow the same pattern of problems namely: never hold them too close or far away (about 10–12 in./ 25 cm is correct), never spray in humid, damp, foggy weather otherwise the paint will go milky, and always spray in light, even, coats—not one heavy application, otherwise it will run and dribble.

Aerosols are cans of paint under pressure. The paint is well thinned, and the propellant is an inert gas—usually freon. Always shake for the recommended time, until the steel ball bearing agitator starts to rattle, then carry on shaking for a further two minutes. This is vitally important to make sure that all the settled pigment is dispersed in the solvent.

For touch-up purposes, aerosols are a complete waste of money. Instead, always try to buy—if available—the touch-up cans with the little brush in the lid. If unavailable, then obtain the correct colour aerosol and, after shaking, spray a little into the can lid and use a small toy paint brush to do the touch-up job. This way saves paint and clouds of overspray everywhere, and concentrates on the chipped spot.

Aerosols do not match all that well, especially metallics. Forget all that drivel about their being factory matched, there should be a trades description against this! Aerosols will allow you to touch up a scraped panel with a modicum of success, providing the same make of primer is used, then de-nibbed, and up to six to eight colour coats are sprayed, then wait at least a week before compounding, T-cutting and wax.

I find aerosols invaluable for spraying small items, and for inside awkward engine bays. The spray underseals are now excellent. The range of aerosols is limitless, for just about everything comes in spray form these days, and all

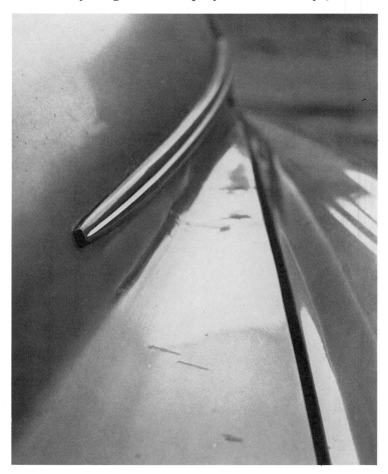

This attempted aerosol touch-up resulted in the wrong colour, and a very rough finish. No attempt was made to prepare and mask up the surface

good accessory shops usually carry not only the body colours, but all the de-rusters, primers, wheel lacquers, engine and exhaust paints (Sperex are the best here—in all colours). Always buy the biggest size available, which will be far more economical in the long run.

If the time arises when an outside body panel has to be re-painted properly, and there has been a high build-up of aerosol spray paint on that panel, then it must be flatted off completely—back to sound original paint, or to bare GRP, or metal. Failure to observe this rule will result in the new paint reacting with the aerosol layers and crazing will occur almost immediately.

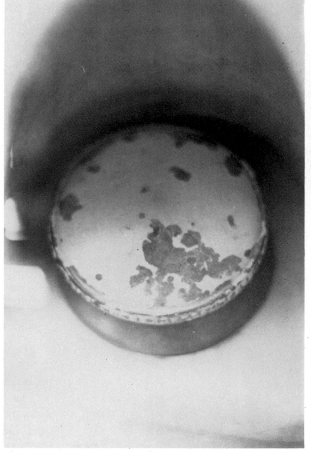

Below right **This chipped filler cap is a suitable piece to repaint using aerosols. All that is required is a good flat back to bare metal then two coats of primer and about six coats of colour. Leave a week, then polish**

Below **Ill-matched aerosol blow in**

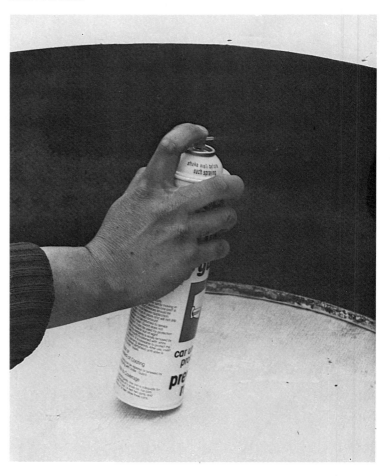

Using a simple aerosol
underbody seal on this Lotus
Seven wing. These aerosols are
excellent for making a clean edge
in wheel arches

Aerosols will keep for a long time if kept cool, and away from direct sunlight and heat. If the nozzle gets clogged, pull it off and dip it in thinners, and have a small pin handy as well. When clear, and if finished spraying, invert the can and spray until nothing comes out i.e. nozzle is now clear. **Never** burn the empty can as the vapour residue will explode the can; this can cause serious injury if anyone is standing close by.

The final paragraph in this section is about colours and mixing schemes. We've all seen the awful colour matches on accident and part-repaired vehicles; why people accept them back in this state I don't know. With all the mixing schemes available, there should be no excuse not to get the colour somewhere 'nearly' right—unless you're colour blind! For the home sprayer, this is a major concern, because the mixing and tinting equipment is not available to you. When you buy the colour take along the fuel filler cap (if colour painted) for comparison, or some part of the body panel, if easily removed, and ask the supplier to match the colour to the sample. Make sure you've T-cutted it first to get the true colour. Hopefully, when you spray it should then be spot on, if not, take it back and ask again. I've sent paint back five times before it was right. If no 'colour' is able to be taken from the car to the paint factors,

Aerosols come in all sizes and colours

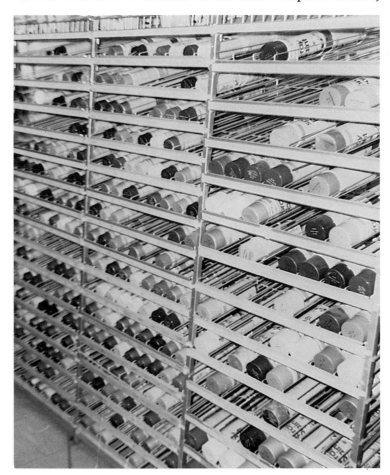

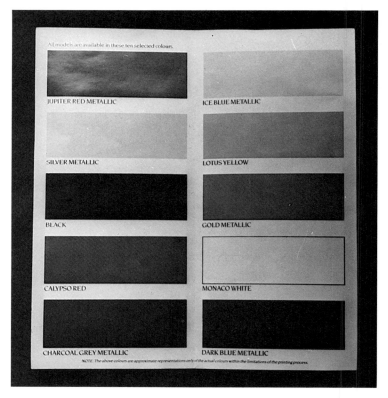

Different manufacturers have different ideas on how to produce colour charts

A small Valentines mixing scheme. The micro-fiche on the right tells the operator what proportions of each tint to use. The paint in the cans is automatically stirred by paddles, and the required amount is then put into the bare colour. This is the automotive equivalent of household mixing schemes

let them have the car if necessary, after all you're paying for the paint, and it's pointless having a 'gold' door on a yellow car. A good paint mixer will take care and is nearly always right but a slap happy couldn't-care-less type will cost you, and the paint factors, a great deal of wasted time and money.

Some paints will change with age, and some old type pigments have been superseded, so when doing part-repairs the new colour **will** look different in certain lights (i.e. artificial daylight and strong sunlight), and nothing can be done to alleviate this.

For full resprays colour choice, if departing from the original, is always personal, but my advice is that light colours will show less marks, and dark colours will highlight every blemish and poor repairs. Black is the very death on badly repaired GRP cars. Whites, too, need some consideration; without going through the list, 'blue whites' will not go off as opposed to 'yellow whites' which will yellow with age. Reds and maroons go off quickly too.

On GRP cars if you are undecided as to what colour to choose, I always recommend white, pale yellow, blue, sand, beige colours or any light colour metallic—(one's eye goes to the metallic fleck not to the bad repairs).

With any dark colours—blues, greens, browns, or blacks—great care should be taken with the final colour coats and the refinishing afterwards.

Chapter 5 | GRP painting

Let's get one thing quite clear before we start. Painting fibreglass is **not** the same problem as painting metal. There are far more problems in achieving a perfect finish on fibreglass than on metal, and, sadly, many professional spray shops just do not have a clue on how to tackle a GRP car. If you are having the car sprayed professionally, go to any specialist firm who sprays GRP cars regularly and understands them; any Lotus, Reliant, TVR or Corvette dealer should know as well. Do not use your friendly chap around the corner whose only claim to fame is that he once did a GRP car, way back in the 1950s, and knows all about them. Put quite bluntly, he does not; technology has changed rapidly since then, and you will have to pay for a finish that will be worse than awful.

What are the problems? Why is it so difficult, and why, to spray a GRP car, properly takes longer (hence more expensive) than a metal one?

1 Basically, GRP is a soft material, as opposed to metal which is hard; this immediately gives problems when repairs have to be made. After the repair is finished and the painting has begun, the thinners can sink into the fibreglass layer, and actually lift the repair edge up—forming the familiar sink mark around the repair—or the thinners can be absorbed into any exposed mat capillaries, to give problems later on. With metal, once the thinners hit the hard surface they cannot be absorbed.

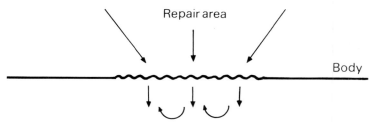

A sequence showing the spray filler being applied to front end damage on a Lotus Eclat. The repaired damage is thoroughly cleaned and dried followed by masking up; note how all the paper edges are taped down. Spray filler is being applied (at 35–40 psi) followed by a dark guide coat to aid flatting down. The helmet type mask with its own air supply is being used

A Lotus Elan +2 awaiting masking up and painting, after a new front section has been fitted

2   It is therefore essential to spend far more time over the repairs in the first place—a GRP repair will take longer to complete than its metal equivalent in any case. A simple gel crack requires grinding, tissue and resin filling to shape, whereas the corresponding metal scrape or tear may need grinding, brazing and filler (or first Davids P40, then filler). Final preparation must be thorough on GRP, for deep score marks left by a rasp file, or P40 or P80 production paper cannot be left, as these will show immediately the paint is applied, because the thinners carry the paint into the mark and keep on going. The more paint is applied, the worse it becomes. All score marks must be removed on GRP, going down to 220 wet-dry paper to achieve a perfect repair/ paint edge when using spray filler, down to 320 and 600 paper when using hi-build primers.

3   The whole painting process takes longer. At the least allow a minimum of four weeks turn-around for a full re-paint. The paint must be allowed to stand, so as to allow any thinner/paint interaction to take place. By smothering the body in primers and colour in a week, or two-week, period the result will no doubt look superb for precisely a month, then all the repairs will show through one by one as the high concentrate of thinners starts

to show. If you are using a synthetic paint, the plastic film will creep into the repair and follow every blemish.

Our schedule is a ten-week turn around comprising:

Spray filler	1st coat	leave 1 week
	2nd coat	leave 1 week
Primers	2 coats	leave 2 weeks
Colour	4 coats	leave 1 week
International Flowline	Final coats	up to 2 weeks
Cellulose system	4 coats	leave 1 week
	4 coats	leave 1 week

All this may seem excessive, but then we have no trouble with repairs lifting or sinking. If there *are* any problems, then of course by leaving the car standing for a long time in between coats, we can rectify long before the customer takes delivery of the finished car. It is far cheaper in the long term, to pay a high price to start with, and wait a little bit longer, than to pay for a quick and cheap respray and then watch all the cracks (having been sprayed over—no repair carried out at all) and marks begin to appear before your eyes, and then having the confrontation with the sprayer because you're not satisfied. This appears to

Spray filler applied locally to repairs. It is essential to confine the spray filler to as small an area as possible, otherwise lifting may occur on the original paint surface

This Lola T70 Mk IIIB had all new body sections, the entire body was flatted with 600 paper to provide a key, then spray filler was used. The final result was as near perfection as was possible in diamond white with Monaco green stripes. The total time on the repaint was 300 hours. Seven litres of white were used and one litre of green, with four litres of satin matt black for all the undersides and interior panels

be a lecture but, time and time again, I see money ill-spent on substandard repairs and painting on Elans, Europas, Marcos, TVR and Gilbern cars. Much money has to be spent on rectification. I can only advise, before you start to ask for professional assistance from an accredited source (and if you cannot match the cost don't do it), wait until you can afford it. After all, another year will not matter, the cracks may look unsightly, but at least the GRP doesn't rust. A cheap blow-over to sell it, really makes life extremely awkward for the next owner to try and sort it out.

If you are undertaking the work yourself understand the repair side first then, if still in doubt, ask for guidance.

4   Painting technique is different. If using the cellulose system, most coats have to be 'dusted' on (i.e. being built up dry), with minimal thinner content to help prevent penetration and possible lifting.

5   Paint stripping takes far longer. Paint strippers attack GRP but not metal. Strippers can be left on metal with no harm being done, but if left on GRP the gel coat is softened, and eventually a hole will appear. Paint can be removed by heat on metal, but not on GRP, for obvious reasons. Acid cleaners cannot be used on GRP, nor can solvents to wipe over the stripped body. Always use the water-soluble paint strippers, not the white spirit ones. Mechanical grinders, the use of flap wheels, cintride discs, and sanders all have to be used with the utmost care on GRP, *if used at all*, for after one slip with a grinder there's a hole to be repaired. It will take at least treble the time to paint-strip a GRP car, compared with a metal body shell.

On any Lotus, TVR, or Reliant Scimitar allow between 70–80 hours to remove up to six layers of paint.

The overall time to spend on stripping, repairing and repainting a GRP car should be, if done correctly, around 200–250 hours; it is now no wonder that the cost is high.

Chapter 6 | Painting self-coloured GRP

This chapter falls into two categories—self-coloured GRP bodies that require a repaint because of age (gel coat colour has gone dull, milky or separated), bad cracking or accident damage, and those that are new which require a top coat, or a change of colour. Kit cars almost exclusively fall into the latter category.

Many kit car bodies come already supplied in a range of basic colours, or in the clear gel state. Bearing in mind the financial restraints on some owners, an expensive professional respray is way beyond their means, so *as a recommendation only* the quickest and simplest way is to spray with an air drying enamel, for this will give a tough durable finish in service. Taking the International scheme as an example:

1   Thoroughly remove any traces of moulding wax left on the body (in hidden corners etc.), and wipe over the whole body to get rid of oil, dirt, grease and other impurities. Use white spirit for this or International Spirit wipe.

2   Flat the entire body, using 320 wet and dry paper then 600 wet paper, to provide a really good keyed surface. Add a little washing-up liquid to the water. When dry, any missed patches will still show up glossy, so flat these.

3   When thoroughly dry, mask up any parts, if not a bare body, and wipe over with a tack rag or lint-free cloth to remove any dust. Spray the primer, using two coats. Use synthetic prime surfacer. There is no need to pre-treat with a self-etch primer, providing you've made a good key. Leave for a day or so then de-nib with 800 wet and dry paper, wet.

4   When dry, spray two coats of Quickline synthetic enamel. This is an air drying one-pack enamel, which is touch dry at 70 degrees F (20 degrees C) in about half an hour. Wait 10–20 minutes before applying the second coat, sprayed at 50 psi. Allow

to harden overnight, and at least 7 days before using. Petrol and oil additives may stain the paint before it has fully hardened. If this occurs, then the panel will have to be re-done. Another tip is to pre-drill all the fixing holes before painting, because drilling after the paint has been applied may tear the plastic film of the enamel. Wait a full week, at least, before any fixing has to be done. With cellulose paint none of this applies; fixing and fitting up can take place the day after painting.

As a rough guide $2\frac{1}{2}$ litres of enamel should be sufficient and 2 litres of primer for the medium sized kit car. 10 sheets of 320 and 600 wet and dry paper and 3 sheets of 800 paper will be required as well.

The aged or cracked self-coloured body requires far more attention than a new one. The colour goes milky and dull because of the ultra-violet effect of the sun's rays, which degrades the pigment in the gel colour. This is a natural process and cannot be avoided, but lighter colours—white, pale blues, yellows—have a better resistance than the dark blues, browns, greens. Every colour has a light fastness rating number when produced at source, and this gives a guide to the resistance to fading. Overall, any colour should last four to eight years before going 'off'. Apart from kit cars, the most familiar 'volume' self-coloured body is the Lotus Seven S4. All Sevens have wings and nose piece that are self-coloured but the S4 had the whole body done as well. Once the colour has started to go off, then no amount of T-cutting and waxing will help; in fact, by doing this the problem will be accentuated because the top surface is exposed even more, and the sun's rays can penetrate that bit further down. The milkiness will return within a few days.

Taking the Seven as an example:

1 Remove everything that can be taken off—wings, side screens, windscreen pillars, lights.
2 Repair any accident damage or gel cracks as described in my Fibreglass book. Briefly this means: grind out, resin and tissue and filler to shape for cracks, using 300 sq. gm (1 oz) mat for reinforcing and repairing on the underside of accident damage. Treat the top surface as for a gel crack.
3 After flatting off the repairs, flat off the whole body and panels with 320 then 600 wet and dry papers, wet with a little

washing-up liquid. As with the new bodies, it is essential to provide a really good key, especially in the corners and crevices. Discounting the repairs, just flatting down will take between six and ten hours. Finally wash off with clean water, and leather off.

4 When dry, mask up any parts remaining on the car, i.e. heater, master cylinders, and the whole of the interior.

5 The painting procedure can now begin, and is identical to general painting of any fibreglass car. Depending on how many filler patches there are, ICI spray filler may be required first, then the primers (either cellulose or synthetic) then colour. If there are only a few small areas of filler, then use a 'hi-build' primer (International Flowline), and a cellulose stopper for any pinholes showing through the primer. If using the synthetic system, then make sure you use the correct stopper.

Two photographs showing attention to detail, on the one hand the Morris Traveller sill completely stripped of all old paint and re-done. All the wood is set in mastic and new door seals have been fitted. Secondly the door on the Ogle Mini has had all its locks and window frame removed plus all the screws as well. It looks awful to spray over the locks etc. If they won't come off mask them up carefully

With either system spray the primers and de-nib with 800 wet and dry paper, wet. Spray the top coats. With the cellulose system spray four coats and de-nib with 1200 wet and dry paper, wet. Spray another four and do the same, finally spray the last coats. With a synthetic system, spray the two coats as described for the new shells.

Quantities:

	Cellulose	Synthetic
Spray filler	1–2 litres	1–2 litres
Primers	3–4 litres	2 litres
Colour	4 litres + thinners	2½ litres + thinners

Plus wet and dry 320, 600, 800, 1200 papers and a tin of stopper.
6   With the cellulose system, wait a few days and very lightly go over the panels with 1200 wet and dry paper, wet and soap.

This hinge was painted off the car, along with the four holding nuts. The nuts were touched up using a toy brush after fitment, as spanner marks are inevitable in this process

Finally polish with fine compound, T-cut and wax, and the final finish should be like a mirror. With the synthetic system, leave for at least a week before fitting up.

7   Refit. Whilst the painting is being done, also do the windscreen pillars, and brackets for the wings and number plates, either by having these items shot blasted and re-stoved or by repainting them yourself. Refit the wings back with new piping and renew the rubbers where possible; this attention to detail is inexpensive and makes all the difference. New paintwork will always highlight rotten rubbers and bad chrome.

Chapter 7 | Chassis and general underbody painting

The underside of any vehicle takes far more of a pounding than the topside, yet to most of us the main priority is to have a gleaming body and we neglect the rest, when really the finances should be directed to the underside and running gear. When all underneath is perfect, *then* spend the money on having the bodywork attended to. All too often I have seen money wasted (up to thousands of pounds) on superb bodywork when the chassis is rotten, or subframes have corroded away, then the car has to be sold because finances have been drained away, and there is no money left to complete the chassis work.

Underbody sealing is now a huge industry in itself with companies such as Ziebart, Dinitrol, Tricentrol and Black Knight all using wax based sealants as an after protection. It is only recently that car manufacturers have taken to wax injecting sills and panels at source, and this has come about from increased consumer concern for a better product. Perhaps they may last a little longer than previously. The car industry has been extremely slow (built-in obsolescence?) to announce body guarantees up to six years, but these are now being offered.

Chassis protection from the earliest days has usually been red lead (red oxide) followed by a chassis black or a bituminous paint. Suspension parts, too, were either plated (cadmium or nickel) or painted. Up to the 1950s, underbody protection was confined to the painting process itself, so the underside was the same as the body colour. During the late 1950s and 1960s, factory undersealing was classified as an extra and, if specified, entailed the finished car being sprayed with the conventional bituminous underseal. This at least afforded some protection, but

A gutted Morris Traveller. At this stage pay particular attention to the inner wings and treat them well. The roof is aluminium, so if stripping back to bare alloy make sure that the surface is well keyed before re-painting. All side and rear door panels are painted and polished first, then put into place after the woodwork has been fitted

Spraying a wing on the underside before fitment, to ensure that the rust doesn't attack for many years to come. Far easier to do off the car, then re-paint the seam areas after fitting. Finally treat with an underbody sealant or a Waxoyl type compound

depended entirely on the skill of operator to cover the whole underside effectively. Any untreated parts would still rust quickly, and water could seep between the underseal and body causing the metal to fester away. Eventually all that appears to hold a floor pan together seems to be the underseal! The early underseals became hard and brittle with age, and used to flake off. More modern underbody preparations are more flexible, and move with the car. Wax injection systems, apart from those already mentioned—the best-known do-it-yourself compound is Finnigans Waxoyl, which will in fact chase moisture away and attach itself to the metal, thereby totally inhibiting rust formation. If any of these compounds are scratched, the surrounding wax molecules will 'cover' over the area, thus affording complete protection.

How then to tackle underbody painting? There are many ways of course, and the overriding choice factor is one of cost, but by being sensible and working to an orderly pattern, superb results can be achieved that will greatly enhance and preserve the life of the car. The alternatives can be described as follows:

1   The easiest and cheapest way is to have the car steam cleaned, either by hiring a steam cleaner and doing it yourself, or taking it to a commercial station who will charge next to nothing—it takes about an hour. When the car is completely dry, check that all is sound, if not re-plate where necessary. Finally brush or spray on underseal or—better still—spray with Waxoyl, or a similar compound.
2   If a more longer-lasting and higher standard finish is required, almost to concours specification, then every component must be stripped down and refurbished.

If the body, either whole or in part, comes off the chassis— this includes prewar as well as modern machinery—then this must be done because everything is then so simple and easy to get at. Likewise, on detachable subframes.

Once the body or subframe has been removed, strip all components off the chassis. Label everything and store away safely until the time comes to repair or refurbish. The following procedure can now be adopted:

a.   Strip all paint off the chassis, either by very hard work using a wire brush or an electric drill, and/or paint strippers and high pressure hose, or by shot (bead) blasting. The latter is the preferable and makes a far more professional job. Shot blasters can be hired from most tool shops (Gunson make a portable one), along with the correct grade of blasting grit required. Alternatively there are many professional blasters who are geared to do this as their livelihood and the cost is not that expensive. For space-frame chassis, shot blasting is really the best method, since wire-brushing yards of tubing can be an extremely tedious business.
b.   With the bare chassis or space-frame make good any damage, either by plating, or by welding in new tubes of the correct gauge and composition. This is important, as 'beefing up' an area, or using an incorrect material composition, may lead to failure elsewhere later on. If there is any doubt about accident damage or twisting on the chassis then expert advice must be sought, and a new section fabricated and let in. This applies to prewar or rare

unobtainable chassis. On more modern lightweight chassis, if there is any doubt at all the chassis **must be replaced**. Lotus are the main users of a true backbone chassis and nearly all of the Elans and +2s are rusting out, especially on the front uprights. These must not be welded. The replacement chassis are galvanised and guaranteed. Marcos also do replacement chassis (metal), and Caterham Car Sales produce spares for the Lotus Sevens. In the above cases the cost of the new chassis is minimal compared to the damage which may be caused by a bodged old one. If there is any surface rust, treat with proprietary products—Jenolite, Kurust, Trustran—and follow their instructions. If large areas exist, it may be necessary to re-plate.

A new galvanised Lotus chassis. Overpainting is not recommended because the paint will not adhere very well until the galvanising has weathered—which usually takes about six months

Above and opposite **Waxoyling a newly built-up Lotus chassis. Spraying at 40 psi ensures that the oil is blasted into every crevice. All suspension components are treated in the same way**

c.   Repainting of the chassis can be done by repeating the original process, or by using more modern paints and techniques. If the original was a flat black paint of the pre- and postwar era, I can see no advantage in painting it a bright blue high gloss finish. As with all colours it is purely personal but many modern paint finishes (e.g. Hammerite) were not invented and the period chassis effect should be retained.

Make sure the chassis or subframe is free from all oil, grease and dirt, by wiping over with a cloth dipped in thinners or fuel. Apply two coats of red oxide primer, either by brushing or by spraying.

Leave for a few days, then apply the top coats, either by brush or spray. The normal top coat is called Chassis Black—this is a satin matt black, petrol and oil resistant, paint designed especially for chassis and suspension components. International make a good one available in 1 litre or 5 litre sizes; two to four coats are sufficient. If a gloss black or colour is required, then use a one or two pack air drying synthetic enamel, as this gives an exceptional high gloss and is chip and oil resistant. In their early days Lotus used to hand-paint all their spaceframes in Valspar battleship grey enamel, and when the enamel flaked it meant that a crack had appeared in the tube underneath. An alternative is to use Bondaprimer, which is an inert resin based primer instead of red oxide. This is far superior, and will not set up any inter-metal reaction with the chassis since—being resin based—there are no metal particles in it.

Use two coats either by brushing or spraying, then wait two days before overcoating.

Galvanising either cold or hot: Cold can be done by using Galvafroid, very expensive and really not worth it. A hot dip has to be used professionally, or chassis distortion can occur. Paint will not adhere for at least six months. With the Lotus chassis, extra protection can be achieved by applying waxoyl.

Use of high gloss Hammerite and similar compounds instead of chassis black, giving an easy wipe-clean surface: Affords excellent protection on more modern vehicles,

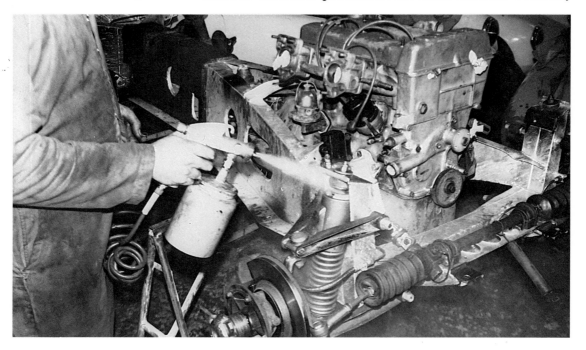

where originality is not the key issue, two or three coats brushed or sprayed is ample.

Finally, the professional spray, whereby, after shot blasting, the chassis is primered using modern high bake polyurethane primers or resin based primers, then stove-enamelled. If this is done correctly, then it is virtually bomb proof and is by far the best way to do all the chassis and suspension components. It is expensive, but the results are well worth while.

A resumé:

Chassis   wire brush
Strip off paint—paint strippers }—Renew
       —shot blasting

Treat rust—Repair if needed

Galvanising—Primer—red oxide—2 coats
            Bondaprimer—2 coats
            Professional high bake primers

Top coats—Chassis black—2—4 coats
          —Air dry enamel—2 coats
          —Hammerite-2—3 coats
          —Professional stove-enamel

(Rust inhibitors—Waxoyl etc.)

Taking the International paint system, red oxide primer is available up to 5 litres, and can be brushed direct from the can, or thinned down to be sprayed.

Chassis black is available as above. If brushing, allow at least three hours between each coat.

Air dry enamel, Nu-Coat agricultural enamel, is available up to 5 litres. One coat only if spraying. Touch dry in two to three hours, hard in eight hours. Available in a range of colours, including black and grey. These enamels are excellent for engine paint as well, there being the grey, dark green and black.

Hammerite is available in all sizes and in a range of colours and Waxoyl is made by Finnigans—obtainable nearly everywhere.

Wooden body framed cars require a thorough checking

Opposite **The wood here has rotted beyond redemption. Replacement is the only answer**

Water has seeped in under the varnish layer to cause the familiar milky staining on this Morris Traveller. This was not too severe and after stripping off all the old varnish (with a sander) the wood was left to dry thoroughly, before giving two coats of Cuprinol, followed by four coats of conventional varnish

over for rot. If there are the familiar black pappy stains at the joints then the only course is to replace the rotten sections. If the structure is sound, then remove any old varnish or sealers by using a sander and/or paint strippers. This can be a time consuming business, and if using paint strippers make sure that all traces are removed, by washing off really well with water—for the water-soluble strippers—or white spirit (Nitromors Original). When thoroughly dry, preserve the frame by dipping it, if possible, in a wood preservative such as Cuprinol, otherwise brush on two or three coats. Modern preservatives like the underseals have improved to an extent that rot is becoming virtually unheard of. If the frame has to be varnished or painted, make sure that all the wood is completely dry, and no 'wet' preservative patches remain, then thin down the first coat with white spirit (50/50), and brush varnish over the whole frame. Likewise with paint. The object of thinning down is to allow the solvent to take the paint into the wood pores. Build up with three or four coats *unthinned*, when the first is completely dry. An electric air-less spray gun can be used, instead of brushing. Varnishes come in all sizes from 250 ml up to 1 litre, and there are straight or polyurethane types. Polyurethane varnishes are tougher in service, and more resistant to oil and petrol, but if moisture gets under the hard surface skin it is trapped, whereas with a conventional varnish the surface can breathe. Two to recommend are John Matthews Spinnaker Yacht Varnish (available at all chandlers) and Ronseal (available at most hardware shops). Ronseal is thinner than varnish and is used on floors and furniture—up to six coats will be required.

The above system can be used for renovating exterior woodwork, 'woodies', and on wooden steering wheels.

Wooden steering wheels, however grubby, can be restored 'as new' by removing all the grease with a solvent (petrol, white spirit), then sanding off all the old varnish with 220 grade followed by 360 and finally 600 papers, all dry. Using a preservative is not necessary, so thin the first two coats down, the first one 50/50, the second 20/80. Build up with three coats, then lightly de-nib with 800 grade paper and varnish a final coat.

Continual overcoating without attention to proper preparation has resulted in this mess. Always mask up the glass area first, to avoid the unsightly dribbles. (These dribbles can be removed by using a razor blade or a Stanley knife blade on its own)

Attention to detail in the shape of new piping after the woodwork has been renewed. Items like this are inexpensive and 'finish' the car. Trying to save, or reclaim, the old is really not economical, and will invariably spoil the final effect

Wood framing and related parts will be discussed in another book; however if your chassis has gone too far it will always be more economical to buy a new chassis or side, and start afresh, than to spend hours on a hopeless reclamation. Many specialist firms cater for prewar and postwar woodwork.

3 Suspension parts, along with the chassis, must be refurbished, so strip off all subassemblies such as the steering arm, trunnion, bushes and swivels, to expose the bare vertical link. Use a variety of wire brushes or an electric drill to remove all dirt, grease and rust. When all is clean, wash off and allow to dry thoroughly, before primering and top coating. Paint as for the chassis. After all components have been painted, then reassemble using new bushes where applicable, and all new nuts and bolts. The use of old nuts—especially Nyloc—can result in components becoming loose again.

Wooden steering wheels can be made to look like new by sanding back to the wood and revarnishing. In this case the rim had five coats of conventional varnish (the first two thinned down 72/25 per cent varnish/ white spirit) and the alloy frame re-polished

If the chassis is being shot blasted, then do all the suspension parts as well (mark off the threaded portions and the mating surfaces). If the chassis is being painted professionally, put the suspension components in with it, for the extra cost involved will be minimal.

If the original component was plated then leave it as it is, and the platers will acid strip the part clean before they re-plate. Most suspension parts were cadmium (either activated or passivated) plated.

Alloy castings deserve a mention, I have never seen a red, blue, yellow or gold painted casting appear as original equipment from a car manufacturer. Again purely personal taste, but all castings should appear as castings. If they are heavily corroded, a very light bead blast will work wonders; followed by a good polish and finally two coats of lacquer (Sperex do one for alloy wheels (Maglac), as do Holts). Alternatively there are chemical cleaners available (Aliclean, Hermetite do a brush on variety, Sperex an aerosol one) that are worked in with a brush and then hosed off.

A resumé of the above:

Suspension parts

Strip assemblies

Steam clean—
Degrease   —
Wire brush   Clean—de-rust
Shot blast   —renew if necessary

Re-plate   —Primer

Top coat—Chassis black
                —Enamels
                —Stove Enamels
                —Hammerite

Reassembly—renew bushes
                —renew all worn parts
                —renew nuts and bolts

(Rust inhibitors—Waxoyl)

4   Non detachable bodies—monocoques, whether metal or glassfibre.

All suspensions and ancillaries will have to be removed from the car, and treated as already described. The underside of the car will then have to be cleaned thoroughly, either by steam cleaning, or with a high pressure hose. To do the job professionally, all traces of underseal should be removed. If the steam clean won't remove it, then paint-stripper and petrol will. It is an extremely messy job. One or two applications of Nitromors water soluble material should be sufficient, and a selection of scrapers (broad knife and the multi-sided scrapers) will help to soften and scrape off. Wiping over with petrol will remove all the little traces left.

If any re-plating needs to be done, now is the time to do it, and then the process of re-painting the underside can begin. Follow the same procedure as for the chassis. The best method if possible is to spray over a pit, and the car supported on axle stands. Spraying is far easier than trying to brush while lying on your back. In addition the force of the spray (at 50 psi) will shoot the primers and top coats well into all the nooks and crannies. Do not forget to mask up the top sides well, otherwise spray drift may end up all along the doors and wings. If appearance is not the issue for originality, then Hammerite is excellent. Finally, spray Waxoyl everywhere on the underside, and if necessary drill holes to get into sills and box sections. A tip here in cold weather is to stand the tin of Waxoyl in a bucket of hot water, as this will make it more fluid. Alternatively, when the car is fully reassembled get it professionally rust-proofed by Ziebart, Dinitrol or equivalent processes.

To stress again, if there is any doubt, especially where safety is concerned, renew but do not patch up holes with newspaper and fillers and then do a superb paint cover up. Many specialist firms make virtually new monocoques, and replacement panels are available.

In some cases, the body itself may be so rotten that in the case of a classic it is often more economical to re-body and start again.

On fibreglass cars most are supplied as the bare mould-ings (as on Reliants and Lotus), and all that is required, if not done at the manufacturing stage, is a coat of under-seal, either by brush or by aerosol or with Schultz gun. If the underside is painted as the body colour (as on the original Lotus Elite) then this must be treated as for doing a full respray. The time taken will be longer here than on painting the top side, as all components must be removed, the car turned upside down, then all oil and muck removed, all cracks damaged made good, all traces of old paint removed, then a good flat down must be tackled and finally the painting process can begin. With an Elite, the total time spent on an underside alone can be up to 150 hours.

This section has taken up many pages, but it is important ot understand that the underside of the car is the first and the worst to suffer and the most time consuming job to do of all, but one done (hopefully) to the highest standards. It should not have to be done again for many, many years and also gives pleasure to look at every time you're under the car.

The only way to do a thorough preparation on the underside is to turn the body upside down, as on this Lotus Elite. Note that the top sides have been stripped of paint using paint stripper—the remaining paint is now removed by hand to avoid damaging the gel coat

Chapter 8 | **Wheels**

Many superb resprays are spoilt by lack of attention to detail, but a shabby set of wheels really does ruin the over-all appearance. As wooden artillery type wheels are outside the scope of this book, three types remain, wire wheels, standard pressed steel and the alloy wheel in all its forms. In all cases it is more beneficial to remove the tyres and valves first but if you are working on a budget, mask around the edge of the rim with masking tape.

Standard steel wheels: The procedure is the same whether they are painted (usually up to early sixties) or stove enamelled (later) in grey/silver. Remove all loose paint and rust with a wire brush, or an electric drill, flat off with 220 followed by 360 wet and dry paper, wet, until the surface is perfectly smooth and thoroughly dry. Mask up if tyres are still in place.

Primer is applied (two coats will be sufficient) either by spraying as for a respray, or by aerosol cans (Holts grey primer, Spectra grey Duplicolor etc.), or by using an air-less electric spray gun that can be hired. When dry, denib with 800 wet and dry paper, wet, thoroughly dry, then apply the top coats of colour either by spraying cellulose or an air drying enamel, or by using an aerosol of the cor-rect colour. If using cellulose or an aerosol up to six coats will be sufficient, with the enamel one good coat is all that is required. For metallics—i.e. gold or silver wheels—use the base coat and clear system. Aerosols are just about suf-ficient, but give a much flatter finish; however this can be overcoated with a clear lacquer to achieve the high shine.

If the wheels have the later stove enamel finish, then the only way to remove the enamel, and get down to the bare steel, is by bead blasting and then re-stoving. If the soiling

This wire wheel is badly corroded and many spokes are loose. A full rebuild is necessary on safety grounds alone

is slight then a good flat with 360 wet and dry paper, wet, then primer and spray one good coat of air drying enamel. Holts Steel Wheels is about the only tough aerosol paint that will do instead of spraying.

Professional stove enamelling is by enamel sprayed on conventionally, then baked in an oven. The enamel will be rock hard after 30 min. at around 80 degrees C.

Wire wheels: follow the same procedure but if there are any loose or badly rusted spokes **do not** overpaint for the wheel must first be re-trued, and new spokes fitted. Never chrome old spokes; if you require chrome wire wheels then dismantle the wheel, chrome the hub and rim and refit with **new** chrome spokes. No reputable plater will chrome old spokes as the process weakens them considerably, and under load they may fail. To paint the wheels, clean thoroughly, either by steam cleaning or use degreaser plus hose, dry then a light flat with 360 paper, prime and paint using aerosols or spray equipment. For stove-enamelling it is far better to let the professional wire wheel specialist do the job properly.

A full service to replace spokes where necessary, re-tension and re-true, bead blast and re-paint or re-stove will work out far cheaper than a new set (if obtainable) of wire wheels.

Alloy wheels are the most sought-after sales accessory and usually costly too. When new they are superb but after one winter the familiar patches of corrosion have set in under the lacquer, and are caused by the salt on the roads.

For any patch of milky lacquer, caused by the film being broken, and moisture seeping underneath, remove all the lacquer by flatting with 360 then 600 paper. When all traces have gone, re-polish the wheel and finally spray three or four coats of clear lacquer (Sperex, Maglac etc.) over them. To do a full set is a time consuming process.

With uniform light pitting due to salt, a thorough rub with a Brillo pad may suffice, if not use 360 followed by 600 paper with plenty of washing-up liquid in warm water. Polish and re-lacquer.

If there has been heavy corrosion, where salt has actually eaten into the alloy, then bead blasting is the only answer,

A similar wheel having had the treatment. It has been professionally rebuilt with new spokes, then bead blasted and finally stove-enamelled. If the spokes are correctly tensioned, then similar results may be achieved by a thorough cleaning and repainting either by spray gun or an aerosol using a polyurethane finish (tougher than cellulose)

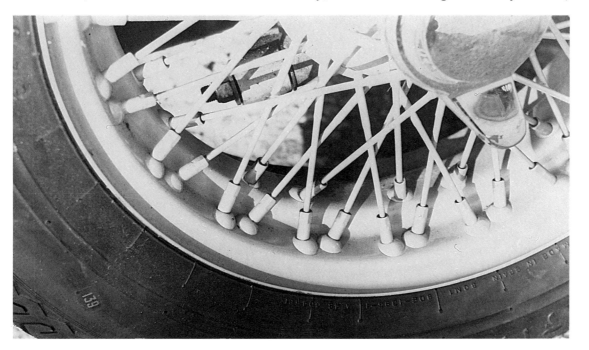

Above **The before and after of an alloy wheel. This was professionally bead blasted, then hand polished and finally lacquered. If the wheels are too far pitted by corrosion, then bead blasting is the only answer. To do the job properly, always take the tyres off**

Tyre paint (dressing) gives a satin sheen to the tyres. This will not harm the rubber in any way, and greatly enhances the overall effect after a respray

The final overall effect of a 'new' wheel, the wheel itself rebuilt and repainted, the tyre finished off with tyre black and also the spinner re-dressed and re-chromed. Attention to detail always 'makes' a car

followed by polishing and lacquering. Another major cause of alloy wheel corrosion is the wrong use of balance weights. **All** alloy wheels should use the special stick on weights, and **not** the usual lead knock-on types, which set up a metal interaction with salt acting as a catalyst. Alloy wheel rims can actually break away taking the lead weight with them because of the severe corrosion set up by the weight.

If the alloy wheels are painted, then follow as above substituting colour for the lacquer. If the wheels are a metallic colour or gold or silver, then spray two or three coats of clear lacquer to finish off.

Finally, to show the wheel off to its full advantage the tyres can be blacked by brushing on a coat of tyre black (Holts or International from 250 ml to 5 litres). This dries in about 15 min to a satin matt sheen finish. The paint does not harm rubber and will not crack-up.

The tyre lettering can be picked out with special tyre paint sticks, usually in white, yellow or gold.

Soiled wheels do take many hours work to reclaim, but once done and kept that way, they will enhance the overall appearance of the car.

Chapter 9 | Coachlining and decals

I believe the art of coachlining appeared on farm wagons long before the advent of the coaching era. Wagons were painted in a set pattern and colours to denote in which county they belonged. True coachlines appeared on the mail and passenger coaches, to highlight and decorate the beautiful woodwork in the 18th century, and with the coming of the motor car the coachlining continued, as most early bodies were pure coaching types on four wheels. The bespoke body builders (James Young, Mulliner, Park Ward and others) used coachlines to highlight various aspects of their designs, and with the introduction of mass production the coachline from the thirties slowly disappeared.

The painted coachline was superseded by tapes, and the tapes superseded by acres and acres of sticky decals and lining—such is fashion! To me this is a great pity, since a well painted thin coachline in the right place can enhance the body line of the car, or complement a colour.

The painted coachline is simple to apply; first of all, wash and dry the 'line' area, then remove all the wax or traffic filth by T-cutting along the proposed line. Polish off and this will provide a key, as well as cleaning the area, for paint will not stick to waxy surfaces very well. You will have to buy the special lining tape, which is a very thin cellophane type strip, available from paint factors. This is placed on the car and then the centre strip is pulled away leaving the two outer pieces perfectly parallel to each other.

With masking tape, the edges of the line would be too rough, and of course over a car's length to create an $\frac{1}{8}$ in. strip with two lengths of tape would be impossible. The lining tape is available from most paint factors, and the

Left **A modern type of 'fashion' striping on a Talbot comes as one-piece, with double sided backing strips**

Below **A painted coachband with TVR being left in the body colour. Coachbanding with contrasting colours can be very effective, and greatly enhances the body lines**

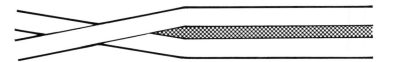

centre section varies in width to suit personal tastes.

To make a pointed finish of the line at the end of the run: after the centre has been pulled away, very gently pick up the two strips left and cross them over at an angle then smooth back down.

Pulls away

Finally with a toy brush (of good quality), paint in the line with unthinned paint, don't go over the remaining tape for obvious reasons. When this is completely dry very gently remove the two strips, and you'll be left with a perfect coachline. After a few days give a good waxing over the original T-cutted area and the new line. A word of warning—make sure the line is compatible with the paint on the car, i.e. if cellulose finish use cellulose for the line, if synthetic use synthetic. Don't mix them up.

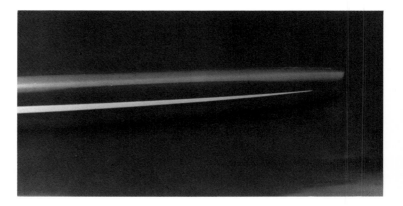

An example of a painted coachline using the special lining tape, the pointed end has been beautifully done on this Morris Minor 1000

There is a stripping kit available from Holland which contains a paint cartridge and a roller wheel and with the aid of a magnetic guide you can produce the perfect line. The kit is expensive for the one-off paint job but could be useful if lining a custom car or hot rod. The address is given in the appendix.

Sign writing can be left to the professional or—by taking great care in mapping out the wording—can be done at home. As for lining, the area to be sign written must be prepared in the same way. Then mark out the wording with a soft leaded pencil, ruler and tape measures. Depending on the size of the wording, choose a suitable width brush and paint in the letters or script—being very careful at the edges. When all has been done leave the job for a few days, then give it a good wax—any pencil markings will be removed with the waxing. On large letter areas or designs, patterns can be made with stencils, and the paint sprayed on.

Tapes and decals are the modern replacement, and these fall into two main groups, the Fablon type line or decal (a plasticy top surface with a peel off backing strip), and the newer lines or decals which have a top and bottom peel off strip, so the decal is sandwiched in between.

In both cases, the area to receive the line or decal must be thoroughly clean and wax free, so after washing, T-cut and polish off. The car and decal must be at room temperature (preferably about 20 degrees C), because trying to stick anything in the cold of winter will be imposs-

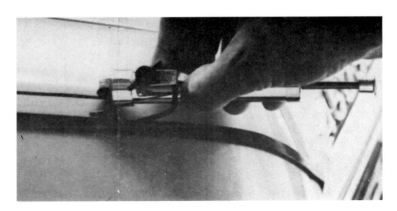

The stripping tool available from Beugler in Holland

As distinct from a painted coachband, the Sunbeam Lotus uses decals. This is extremely difficult to fix due to the width, for all air bubbles must be smoothed out as you go along. Essential to apply at room temperature 20–25 degrees C. Repeated lifting off to align correctly will only stretch the decal, and sometimes damage will result

ible, as the adhesive goes hard and the plastic layer becomes brittle. The end result will be a broken decal, that will not stick at all well. If it is not possible to achieve an overall degree of warmth, do not attempt to grill the area locally with a heater as the decal will expand and of course stick very well, but when the heat source is removed the decal will shrink back and peel off. With the single backing strip type peel a feel inches off (if a line), and press the edge of the tape firmly onto the vehicle, use a firm pressure to smooth all the air bubbles out, continue peeling off the backing strip and smoothing down as you go. With the top and bottom strips, if a coach line, do as above, then when all is in place, gently pull the top strip off. With a decal remove the backing strip completely if it is a short name, then stick onto the car smoothing away any trapped air bubbles, then gently pull away the top strip. On longer decals do as for the lines. Some of the names (e.g. Lotus, Eclat, 2.2) are very fragile once the backing piece is peeled away because of the delicate nature of the design, and great care must be exercised on this type.

Adhesive number plates are fitted as for single type tapes. Make sure no air is trapped underneath, fix the plate on first, then the letters.

In all the above cases do not wax over until at least a week has passed, because the solvents in the wax may attack the new adhesive. Decals by the fuel filler neck may

A signwriter's nightmare, the lettering is all painted—not done by transfers. For any F1 car the signwriter can take up to two days to hand write a new model

Continual spillage of fuel is causing the staining and slight lifting at the rim edge. The fuel will attack and darken the adhesive. Nothing can be done except to renew the decal

A car park scrape resulted in the decal being badly scored. Silver paint (silver decal) would hide the mark for a short term answer, but in the long run a new decal is the only answer

The Lotus Eclat decal is extremely delicate, and great care must be ex ercised when applying. Made by 3M, this has top and bottom backing strips

become badly stained after a period of time. This is due to spilt fuel attacking and staining the adhesive, which in turn stains the plastic layer. Nothing can be done apart from replacing the decal—and careful refuelling in the future!

To remove any line or decal, the procedure is the same. Lift up one end and carefully pull away, especially with number plates, for one sharp tug may pull the paint away with it. Do not attempt removal on cold days, as the decal will break because it is brittle. Get the car warm if possible, if not go along the decal or the line with a hot air hair dryer or fan heater. Once it is thoroughly warm it will peel off fairly easily. On hot sunny days no extra heat will be required. If any pieces are left use your thumb and roll the bits off, and if any adhesive is left, wipe gently with a cloth moistened in fuel or spirit wipe (International). Do not use anything sharp such as a chisel or screwdriver as you'll damage the paint.

Decals that have been put on the vehicle and have been forgotten will have stained the paintwork underneath by now. A compound, T-cut and wax may help, but normally the only course of action is a good flat off and repaint. If the decals are unwanted, do remember to remove them as soon as the event is over.

Chapter 10 | Waxing

The paintwork may be sound but has dulled or faded with age, the colour may look a bit milky, and a respray is out of the question. The use of a colour restorer is an answer to the problem. Car Plan T-cut is the most well-known, it was the first, and most probably is still the best. All the colour restorers available are really mildly abrasive chemical cleaners. They are not waxes, and after application the vehicle must be waxed immediately. The chemicals dissolve the grime, oil films and the abrasive agents remove the top layer of paint, which explains the colour coming off on the cloth. Maroons, some yellows and dark browns are the worst for fading—maroons are exceptionally soft finishes.

If the paintwork is exceptionally dull then a T-cut may not be sufficient and first a compounding will be required.

Rubbing compounds are really varying grades of sand suspended in a weak ammonia solution and are applied by hand, or by a mop. ICI, International, and most paint suppliers, make their own compounds and they range from either fine, medium, to coarse, or have a number from G1 to G7, 1 being ultra fine and 7 being coarse. They vary in consistency too, some are very creamy (the most beneficial) to others which are very runny and 'grainy' (these are awful). Sizes range from 250 ml up to $2\frac{1}{2}$ litres and 5 litres. The procedure is the same for refinishing a car after spraying, as for rectifying old tired paint. Professionally, compounds are applied by large lambswool mops of 10 in. diameter spinning round at speed on power tools. In the wrong hands, these can be extremely dangerous, and can remove all the paint on sharp radii and edges. One can use a 5 in. mop on an electric drill attachment set on a low

Above A professional mop, and a can of rubbing compound. When a mop reaches this stage a new one must be fitted. The mops are lambswool and usually two or three are required per vehicle repair

Left Using a professional 10 in. mop. Note the flat angle of attack. In the wrong hands havoc can be wreaked by the mop spinning at 200 rpm, removing all the paint from sharp edges and around openings such as doors

speed, keeping the angle of attachment as flat as possible. This will take a long time to go over a whole car. By hand also takes hours, but may be the safest way.

Always buy the best quality polishing cloth (which is known as mutton cloth). Don't be tempted to buy cheap synthetic rolls, as these contain harsh nylon strands that will scratch the paint badly. Start with a medium compound, and experiment on a part that won't show. If the colour comes off too drastically, then buy a finer compound, or if nothing happens at all then go to a coarser one. Two golden rules that apply to all compounding, T-cutting and waxing are: First: always rub in the direction of the panels in **straight movements. Do not rub in circles.** Do not go across the panel.

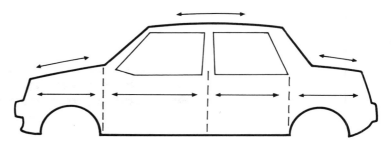

Second: always apply an even pressure on the cloth. The reason for straight movements by hand is that you cannot re-create a mop spinning at high speed and if you rub in circles these will show on the paintwork and reflect the light at all angles, whereas in straight lines, the light is reflected in one plane only. When the correct grade of compound has been selected, start on the roof and work down. Make a generous pad of cloth, and rub gently at first, then apply harder pressure if necessary. Don't try too hard as the compound will dig in and mark the surface. Rub the area until the compound is all but off and a shine is starting to come back, then immediately follow up with a fresh cloth, removing all traces of the compound. Do this because compound left on the surface will dry, leaving the sand behind in a dry paste, and this can be a nightmare to remove. When the roof or complete panel is done, I would advise T-cutting and waxing immediately. Apply

T-cut on a new piece of cloth, under even pressure until the T-cut has gone, then follow up with a new piece, buffing up to a high shine. To T-cut correctly takes hours and many people slop it on, and then give a cursory wipe over, to leave the residue to go milky on the car. Wax immediately, as T-cut is not a wax, and the cleaned surface now requires protection. Use a non-abrasive wax—many are available, either in solid cream or liquid form. Waxes like oils are a personal choice but I always recommend that you use a good one like Turtle Wax. Apply the wax in straight lines and allow to dry and buff off immediately. The paintwork should now be nearly as new.

Some general points:

a. Never apply compound, T-cut or wax in direct sunlight or heat (i.e. outside in a hot summer) because once baked on you will never get it off. Remove the car to a shady place, or into the garage, wait until the paint surface is cold (early morning or evening), then dissolve the residue with fresh compound etc. on a cloth, rubbing gently all the time. Immediately, buff off with a clean piece of cloth.

b. Do one panel at a time with the whole process. Don't be tempted to compound the whole car at once, because if time runs out and the car has to be used, then all your hard work will be to no avail as the paint will be unprotec-

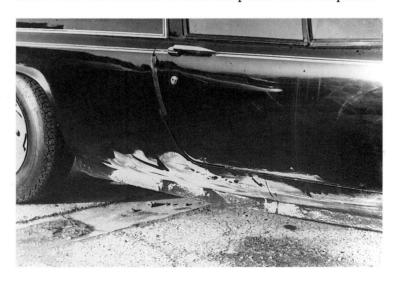

Don't leave T-cut (or wax) unpolished on a car, for this is what happens. The white stain will have to be re-dissolved in more T-cut (or wax) and polished off immediately, then buffed up with a clean dry cloth

ted by a wax layer, and dulling will occur almost immediately.

c.   On a new paint surface, allow to settle for about seven to ten days before compounding for cellulose finishes. **Do not** compound some synthetic enamels as these will change to a dull milky surface. Always check first with the paint supplier, as to the refinishing application. If the surface has deep orange peel, and your compounding makes no impression on it, then a professional buffing may be the only answer, or start with 1200 paper and soap (see earlier).

d.   Always have plenty of fresh cloth and turn it regularly whilst polishing off.

e.   If the compound goes sticky and dries out, add a little cold water and stir in well. Don't over thin.

f.   Some waxes are applied on a damp cloth. If so, immerse the cloth in cold water then wring it out, so that it is just damp, not sopping wet. Follow the instructions on the bottle or tin, as correct waxing is the key to a beautiful shine. Waxing in damp weather may not allow the wax to dry out, and after polishing white smears will remain. Try and choose a dry day outside or get the garage warm. Ideally waxing should be done between 50–70 degrees F (10–20 degrees C).

Quantities are hard to determine for they depend on the state of the paint, but as a rough guide for a medium sized car you will need:

> $2\frac{1}{2}$ litres tin of compound
> 1 litre T-cut
> 500 ml wax
> 1 roll of good quality mutton cloth

It makes more sense to buy larger quantities of T-cut and wax as they are always useful for normal upkeep. It is more economical too, for $2\frac{1}{2}$ litres or even 5 litres sizes will last for years.

Time taken depends on the state of the car at first, but at least a day and a half or two days will be needed to do it correctly. If you take less than a day, then it has not been done properly. Your arms should be aching and feel as though they will fall off—which is another reason always to apply an even pressure throughout.

Chapter 11 | General care of paintwork

Listed below are several hints on how to keep a newly painted car gleaming for years afterwards. Apart from the unfortunate scrapes and dents that we all seem to pick up, there are natural and man-made hazards to be aware of.

Natural hazards: the main one is bird droppings, for these are extremely detrimental to fresh paintwork (especially cellulose) and literally etch themselves into the paint, because of the corrosive chemicals contained in them. It is imperative to wash these off immediately, for even leaving them on the car for a day may cause an unsightly mark when removed. Use plenty of clean water. If they are baked on (especially in summer) soak them for a long time until they can be sponged away. **Do not** scrape off, as this will damage the paintwork. If a mark does remain, try a gentle waxing over the area, and if this fails then a light T-cut and wax will be needed. Cow muck must be well soaked before you attempt to wash it off.

Tree secretions cause a problem, and lime trees are the most prevalent. The sticky fluid that covers the car when parked under the trees is the nectar that is secreted from the leaves. These will not harm the paintwork but should be washed off as soon as possible with warm water, otherwise dirt and general grime will be trapped on the sticky surface. The heavier resin secretions of coniferous (pine) trees do cause a problem, in that they can be extremely difficult to remove because of their general stickiness, and if left they can etch into the paint. The best way to deal with this is with very hot water with a little washing-up liquid added, and keep using a clean piece of sponge until all the deposit has gone. When dry, a light waxing is essential.

Sea spray and winter salt must be washed off immediately, as this leaves a sticky film all over the car. If left, salt will absorb moisture from the air and the car is permanently 'wet'. When the air is dry the characteristic white film of salt crystals are seen on the bodywork (noticeable on dry days in winter time). Salt is the worst accelerator of rust and if left unwashed for days will speed up the process on any unpainted parts; it always pays to wash off salt immediately both on top and underneath the car as well. If the car has to live by the sea, then two good waxings a year, and more frequent washings will keep it in shining condition for a long time. Extremes of temperature should be avoided until the paint has settled down—normally about three months. If caught out in freezing weather, and heavy deposits of ice are on the car, allow them to thaw out naturally; do not scrape ice or snow off the body, as this will scratch the paint. Allow the heat of the engine and interior heater to thaw off the ice.

With excessive heat and direct sunlight try to park in the shade; if this proves impossible you should cover the paintwork with white sheets, and leave some windows open in order to circulate some air. On black and dark colour paintwork the surface temperature can reach as high as 80 degrees C (180 degrees F). Paint problems will occur at this temperature and on GRP cars the resin will deform at around 140 degrees F. In the UK surface temperatures as high as this are extremely rare but in other parts of the world (USA, Middle East, Australia) they are fairly commonplace.

Man-made hazards are numerous and are to be avoided at all costs. The worst for new paint is road tar. If the car is to be collected from the painters in summer, and the road home is being re-surfaced, turn around and find another way home! If tar is on the car, then immediately remove it with a proprietary solution (Holts market one) or use white spirit or petrol on a clean piece of soft rag. Use sparingly—then when all the tar is off, wax well. If the new paintwork is chipped by stone chippings, then the only answer is to flat off and repaint. Most fuels contain harmful additives that, if spilt on the bodywork, may attach and cause severe staining. The stain may usually be removed by a very light T-cut and wax. If this fails, then the panel will have to be repainted.

Cement dust and droppings are a common occurrence if the car is parked by a building site. Treat as for bird droppings, and wash with copious quantities of water. Cement contains lime (alkali) and this will cause an unsightly stain if left alone.

Chemicals wreak havoc with fresh paintwork, particularly paint strippers, brake fluids, thinners, antifreeze, and some gear oils. Brake fluid accidents are the most common.

The additives in fuel have completely removed the new paint, and the area has deteriorated rapidly, leaving rust pock marks. The panel should have been flatted immediately after the attack, and re-painted, not left to get to this state

Always buy the best possible chamois leather, as large as feasible. This one was four square feet when new

When bleeding the brakes or clutch, cover all round the master cylinder area with a sheet then paper on top, and take care. If fluid is spilt wash it off **immediately** with water; if none is to hand try spitting on it, for it must be neutralised, otherwise it will soften the paint and bubble it up. If this does happen then, sadly, the panel will have to be repainted.

It always pays to have the local area on the car protected when you are working with chemicals, also have the neutralising agent to hand. Paint stripper, brake fluid, and antifreeze require water, some oils require petrol, others like thinners, easy-start carburettor and brake cleaners in aerosol form require solvents that attack the paintwork anyway, so protection here is essential otherwise it will necessitate a repaint. If any chemical is spilt on the protective covers then wash these immediately as well, otherwise the next time you cover the car you'll wonder how the paintwork has become blistered.

Industrial fallout: To illustrate this, a friend of mine had a brand new Mini Cooper in white and beige and within two months of ownership the roof had pink smudges all over it. The roof was resprayed under warranty, but within two months the same had happened again. After a battle with the supplying dealer, the cause was eventually found; he was parking his car near a power station, whose chimneys were pouring out 'acid rain'. The chemicals in this fallout were detrimental enough to alter the white pigmentation on the roof to pink. The roof had to be stripped back to bare metal, and re-done and he then used to leave the car at home and used the train. If situations arise like this, and it is impossible to leave the car at home, try and park up-stream of the wind direction and wash the car every night. If severe discoloration takes place, then a repaint is the only solution. Sadly too, many industrial processes still belch out harmful soots, tars and acids that attack paintwork and, like salt, accelerate the rusting process.

As discussed earlier, synthetic enamels and acrylics will stand up better to all these hazards than will cellulose, which is a softer paint, but this is not a reason to leave the area unwashed for any length of time.

We all know our own best way on how to wash a car, so I will not insult anyone by telling them how, but a few pointers may help:

Firstly, **never** use detergents, for these are far too harsh for the paintwork. We've all seen cars covered by a mountainous load of suds, which when washed away leave lovely streaky white lines everywhere. Always use a wash-wax preparation (Turtle wash-wax is very good) which has mild detergent agents with silicones in them—they leave your car shining after leathering off. Never wash the car in direct sunlight, especially during summer months when the heat will evaporate the water too quickly, leaving stains—even more especially in hard water areas. Always soften the grime first by a gentle hosing, or with a rose fitted to the watering can.

Don't use a strong jet, otherwise the dirt will be forced into the paint. When all the car is thoroughly wet, then use plenty of warm water with your wash-wax in it and go over the entire car, not forgetting the door shut faces. Rinse off thoroughly, so that no suds remain, and leather

Above **A concours winning Morris Traveller in Almond Green with all the woodwork refurbished alongside its stablemate waiting to receive its total strip down**

Opposite **The use of colour is important as on this rare Broadspeed Mini. The paint scheme should be a silver roof over metallic regal red, and by having it the wrong way round the car looks even more squashed and dumpy than it really is. Having the darker colour on top of any car will always appear to flatten or lower it**

off. Two points: firstly, always buy a good sponge, for some sponges are cheap synthetic blocks of pure rubbish that only serve to scratch the paintwork. Secondly: there is no alternative to a quality leather. Always buy the best, for if properly looked after, it will last at least a year. Again, cheap alternatives will not do. A tip on leathering off a car is to lay the leather out and then hold two corners and pull towards you on all flat surfaces—this will leave a perfect streak-free finish.

Car washes are the death for high quality repaints. Quite simple—**don't** use them. They may be just about adequate for a lazy company car driver, but not on a precious classic car. In the same vein, all the feather duster type brushes and anti-static wands that are available are really a waste of time and money. Rubbing a brush over a dusty car only serves to scratch the surface, which if viewed under a microscope would appear like a record disc. There is no substitute for the good old-fashioned wash and leather off.

An effective way for underbody cleaning is to obtain a piece of copper tube, then to flatten and fan out the end. Fit the other end to a hose and there is a forceful fan spray jet that can get in under wheel arches. If the hose is $\frac{1}{2}$ in. bore (13 mm) then a 12 in. length of $\frac{1}{2}$ in. tube is ample.

Appendix | Flowline: Cellulose Car Colour

Description

This is a nitro-cellulose enamel for cars and light commercial vehicles of metal or fibreglass construction. It can be used on nitro-cellulose, acrylic or stoved synthetic finishes but not on air dried synthetic coach finish.

Flowline Cellulose Car Colour is available in a wide range of colours through the International Paint Flowline Mixing Scheme and also in a range of ready mixed colours.

Surface preparation

(i)   It is essential to apply Flowline Cellulose Car Colour to a properly prepared surface.

(ii)   Clean the surface to be painted with International Wax and Grease Remover.

(iii)   Wet flat with Grade P600–800 paper.

(iv)   Wash off residue and dry thoroughly.

(v)   Reclean with International Wax and Grease Remover.

(vi)   Prime as required with Surfacer 22 or Supafil, Cellulose Primer Fillers.

(vii)   Wet flat primed areas using Grade P600–800 paper.

(viii)   Remove residue and dry thoroughly. Then reclean with International Wax and Grease Remover.

Thinning

Approximately 1 volume Flowline Cellulose Car Colour, 1 volume thinner (as applicable).

Thinners

Flowline Fast Thinner 86.
Flowline Very Fast Thinner 88.

Flowline Colour Thinner 35.
Flowline Non-Bloom Thinner 37.

Application
Spray full wet coats to achieve opacity, allowing flash-off between coats.

Number of coats
3 minimum.

Spraying viscosity
21–24 seconds BS Cup B4 at 21 degrees C.

Air pressure
50–60 psi.

Drying time at 18 degrees C
5 minutes between coats using Flowline Very Fast Thinner 88.
10 minutes between coats using Flowline Fast Thinner 86.
15 minutes between coats using Flowline Colour Thinner 35 or Flowline Non-Bloom Thinner 37.
All touch dry in 15 minutes.
All hard dry in 4 hours.
These times are dependent on film thickness, humidity and shop temperature.

Special notes
When dealing with an unknown finish it is advisable to test a small area with Flowline Cellulose Car Colour. If pickling or wrinkling occurs, the existing paintwork must be stripped, or sealed with International Isolator. When matching aged paintwork it is possible to reduce the gloss of Flowline Car Colour by adding up to 15 per cent (by volume) of International Matting Base to Flowline Cellulose Car Colour prior to thinning and application.

Health and safety
Use in well ventilated conditions and away from naked flames.
Do not smoke while using this material.

Avoid contact with the skin and eyes. If contact occurs with the eyes, give prolonged irrigation with water and get medical attention immediately.

Subject to the Petroleum (Consolidation) Act 1928 and the Highly Flammable Liquids and Liquefied Petroleum Gases Regulations 1972 concerning use and storage.

Flash point
Flowline Cellulose Car Colour, below 22 degrees C.
Flowline Fast Thinner 86, below 22 degrees C.
Flowline Very Fast Thinner 88, below 22 degrees C.
Flowline Colour Thinner 35, below 22 degrees C.
Flowline Non-Bloom Thinner 37, below 22 degrees C.

Paint suppliers

All aerosols can be obtained through motor accessory shops such as Halfords. All stock similar products from the various manufacturers, notably Holts, Dupli-Color, Sperex, Spectra, and Comma. All paints and associated products are available through local trade factors throughout the U.K. such as Brown Brothers and Affiliated Factors. All paint manufacturers usually have a technical department, and their address is usually printed on the tin. The two major ones listed in this book are:

International Vehicle Finishes
Rotten Park Street
Ladywood
Birmingham B16 OAD.   Tel: 021 455 9866

ICI Autocolor
Wexham Road
Slough
Berks.

All body fillers are available from trade outlets, accessory shops, the main supplier being David's:

W. David and Son Ltd.
Northway House
High Road
Whetstone
London N20 9LR.   Tel: 01-455 0372

Beugler Stripers
Postbus 122
3971 Le Driebergen
Holland.

Index